THE FACE OF STRUGGLE
AN ALLEGORY WITHOUT WORDS

Seth Tobocman

with an introduction by
Peter Kuper

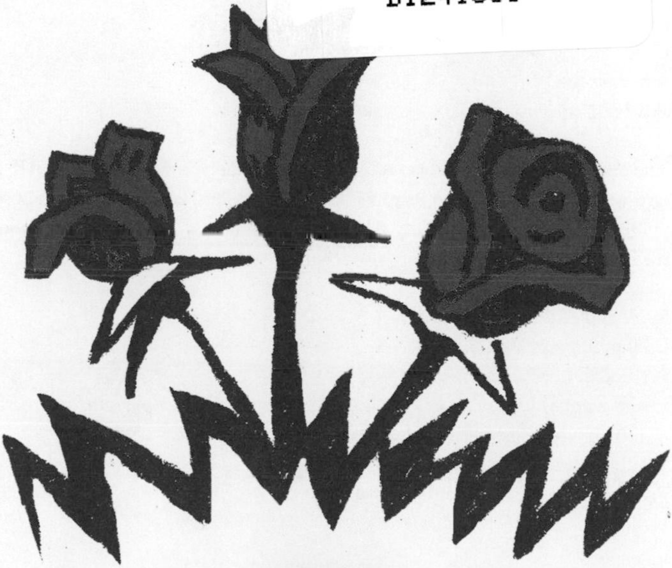

AK PRESS

The Face of Struggle: An Allegory without Words
© Seth Tobocman, 2020
Introduction © Peter Kuper, 2020

This edition © 2020 AK Press (Chico, Edinburgh)

ISBN: 978-1-84935-377-9
E-ISBN: 978-1-84935-378-6
Library of Congress Control Number: 2019947452

AK Press	AK Press
370 Ryan Ave. #100	33 Tower St.
Chico, CA 95973	Edinburgh EH6 7BN
USA	Scotland
www.akpress.org	www.akuk.com
akpress@akpress.org	ak@akedin.demon.co.uk

The above addresses would be delighted to provide you with the latest AK Press
distribution catalog, which features books, pamphlets, zines, and stylish apparel
published and/or distributed by AK Press. Alternatively, visit our websites for
the complete catalog, latest news, and secure ordering.

Story and Art: Seth Tobocman
Inking: Tamara Wyndham
Artmodel: Louisa Krupp
Image from Si Lewen's *The Parade* used by permission. Copyright: International
    Institute for Restorative Practices
Eric Drooker image used by permission
Printed in the USA on acid-free paper

Contents

Louder Than Words

In 1919, the mustard gas from a World War barely dissipated, Flemish artist Franz Masereel published a "picture story" in 167 woodcut images. Titled, *Passionate Journey*, it told the tale of an everyman making his way through the hustle and bustle of the complicated modernizing twentieth-century world and captured the zeitgeist of his time. Masereel's book not only anticipated the advent of the graphic novel, it sold well enough to create interest from publishers in wordless stories and inspire endless artistic followers. Among them was the German artist Otto Nückel who, in 1926, used the dark tale of a woman suffering trials and tribulations of life, as a social critique in his woodcut illuminated *Destiny*. The first American to embrace this form, Lynd Ward, created the wordless book, *God's Man*, published just a week before the 1929 stock market crash. Ward, who said he had to become an artist since his name is "Draw" spelled backwards, told the tale of a young artist who makes a deal with a mysterious stranger. The protagonist is given a pen and artistic success in exchange for a modest price—his soul. The book was a huge hit even as the Depression swept the country.

That same year, Czech printmaker, Helena Bochořáková-Dittrichová produced the coming of age woodcut book *Childhood*. Considered to be the first woman to create a graphic novel, Bochořáková-Dittrichová detailed both the normality of a middle class life and its tribulations as her central character discovers she is going blind. István Szegedi Szüts's *My War*, published in 1931, expressed the Hungarian artist's World War I experience with a poetic darkness. A looser version of the picture story both stylistically—done in brush and ink—and in a less linear narrative form, yet an emotionally powerful account.

Frans Masereel, from *The Passion of Man*

In 1938, the Italian Giacomo Patri created a response to the impact of the Depression in his book *White Collar*. He used his story to address the desperate need for unions, women's access to safe abortion, and the lack of affordable health care for the poor. My, how times have changed.

Frans Masereel, from *Passionate Journey*

Southern Cross, Laurence Hyde's 1951 sequential woodcuts, chronicled the lead up and devastating aftermath of the American military's atomic bomb tests in the Bikini Islands. He vividly portrayed the affects of radiation on the local populace and environment with images that burn into your brain. First published in 1957, Si Lewen's *The Parade* was conceived by this Polish-Jewish refugee from Germany during World War II. Part of an elite G.I. team, he was part of the Normandy invasion and entered Buchenwald immediately following its liberation. The images he created from these experiences, indelibly illuminate the catastrophe of war.

Helena Bochořáková–Dittrichová, from *Childhood*

In the world of comics, one of the fathers of the form, Will Eisner, who coined the term "graphic novel," found great inspiration in the work of Lynd Ward and experimented with text-free story telling throughout his career. This further extended the reach of wordless books as new generations of cartoonists were exposed to the possibilities.

Among the new generation were Seth Tobocman, Eric Drooker, and myself. The pioneers I've enumerated above spoke to us instantly when we separately saw them in high school. Though many of those early artists had fallen out of fashion, for the three of us they were current events when we converged in New York City in the early 1980s.

István Szegedi Szüts, from *My War*

They were in our bloodstream; morse code in pictures, telegraphing to us through time and space and linking us to the history of artistic activism and to one another. They inspired the three of us to try our hand at this ingenious form. From Drooker's graphic novels *Flood!* and *Blood Song*; my own books, *The System*, *Eye of The Beholder*, and *Sticks and Stones*; to Tobocman's short stories "ESCAPEE" and "The History of America and Tompkins Park," we used this image-as-language to share our stories.

Now you hold in your hands Seth's latest exploration, *The Face of Struggle*. In forty-two pages he visualizes nothing less monumental than the rise of a moral leader, the co-opting of her ideas for nefarious ends, and the possibility of overcoming the forces of capitalist greed. With this book, Tobocman joins hands with his predecessors connecting to past battles and how they are reflected in today's events. Though

Si Lewen, from *The Parade*

6

the faces of corrupt politicians may have changed over the years, their diabolical intent remains the same.

Our struggle in the twenty-first century, however, has reached a new critical mass. Autocrats are on the rise worldwide. From Trump to Bolsonaro, they preach national socialism even as they demonize true socialists. The masks worn by these leaders to entice us down the garden path are being lifted for anyone with a pair of eyes, lungs, and

Eric Drooker, from *Flood!*

7

functioning brain. Their greed knows no bounds and their lust for power blinds them to reality—the reality that our home is on fire and they will burn too. We've only got one planet "A" and all the money in the world won't buy them an escape on rocket ships to Mars.

Tobocman's *The Face of Struggle* uses an array of symbols to capture these truths and plugs into a universal language that will not be deterred by border walls. Throughout his career Seth Tobocman has used his powerful art to shake people from complacency. Even when it's without words, his message has been loud and clear for decades: It's in our hands to turn the tide, before the tide turns on us.

Peter Kuper
New York City, 2019

EYE OF THE BEHOLDER
UNITED PAPER CORP.
NEWS
NEWS
NEWS
NEWS
RAINFOREST DESTRUCTION CONTINUES

Peter Kuper, *The Eye of the Beholder*

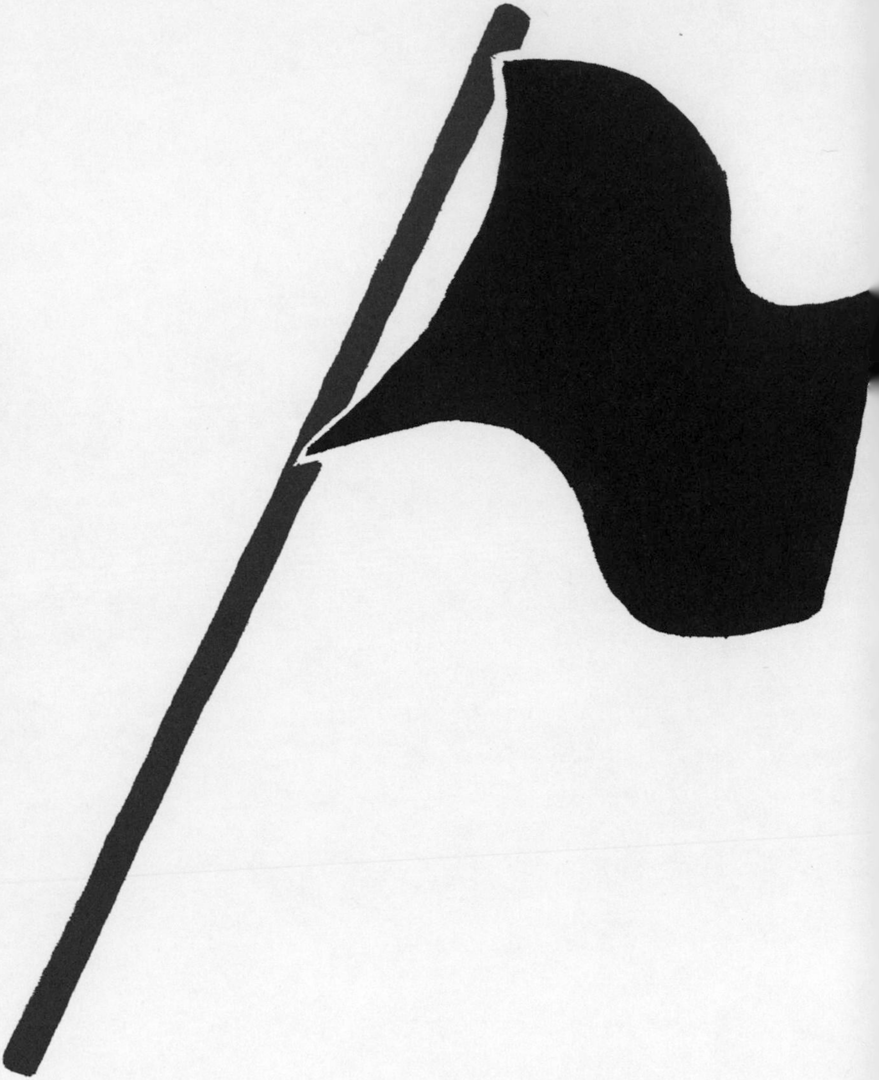

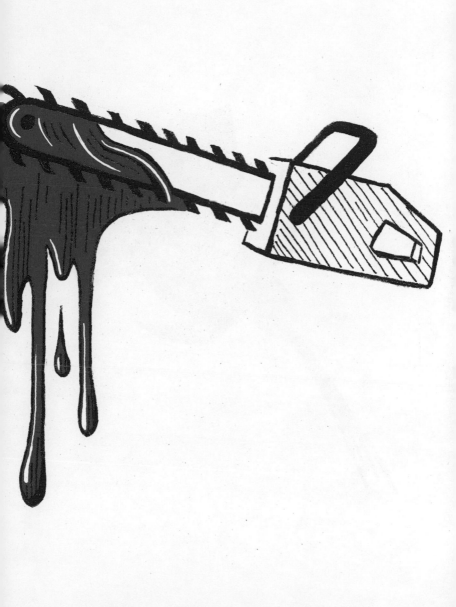

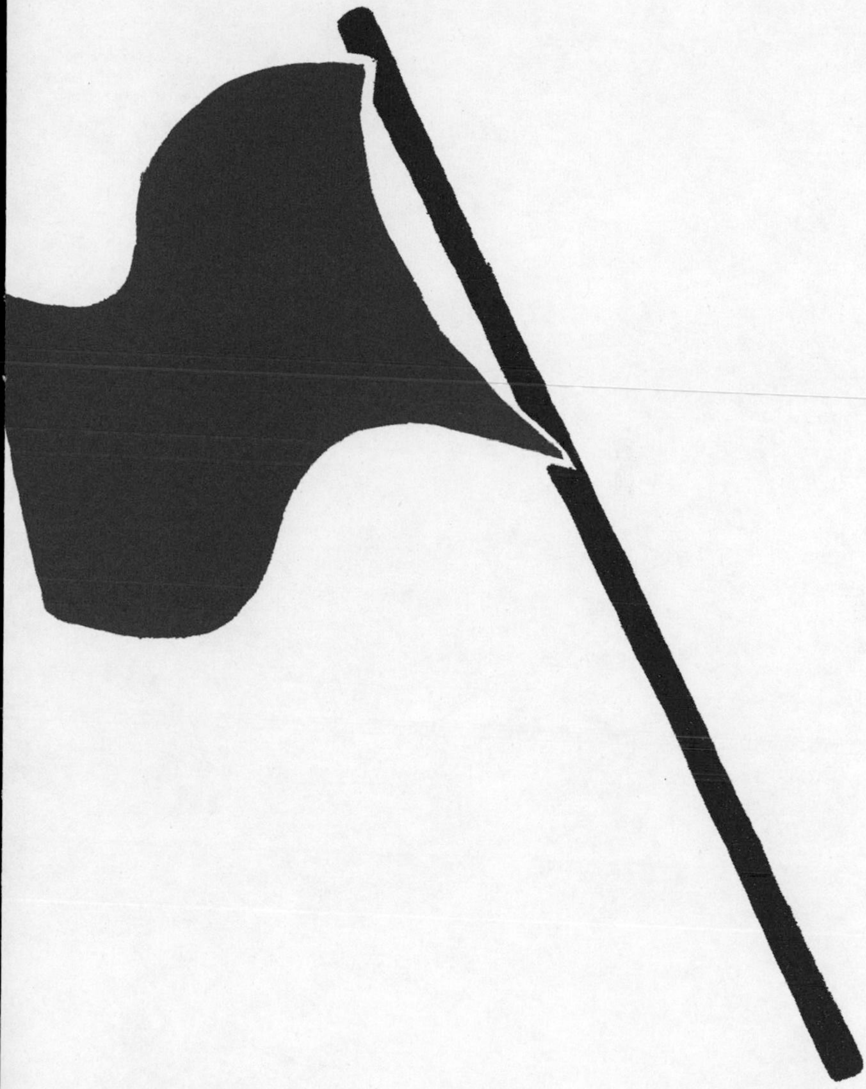

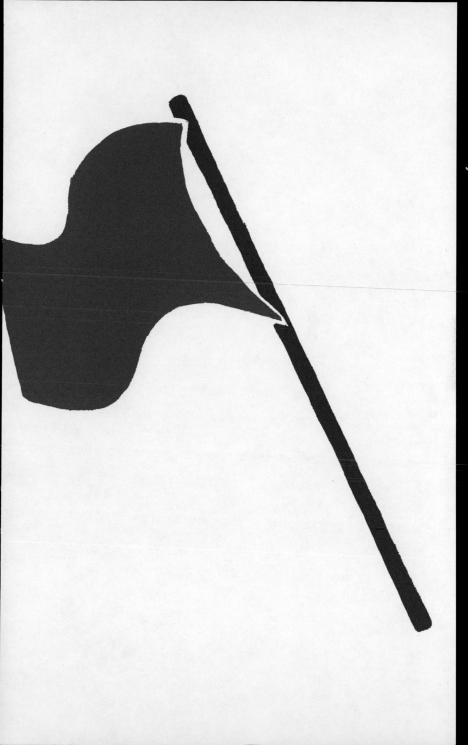

THE FACE OF STRUGGLE
AN ALLEGORY WITHOUT WORDS

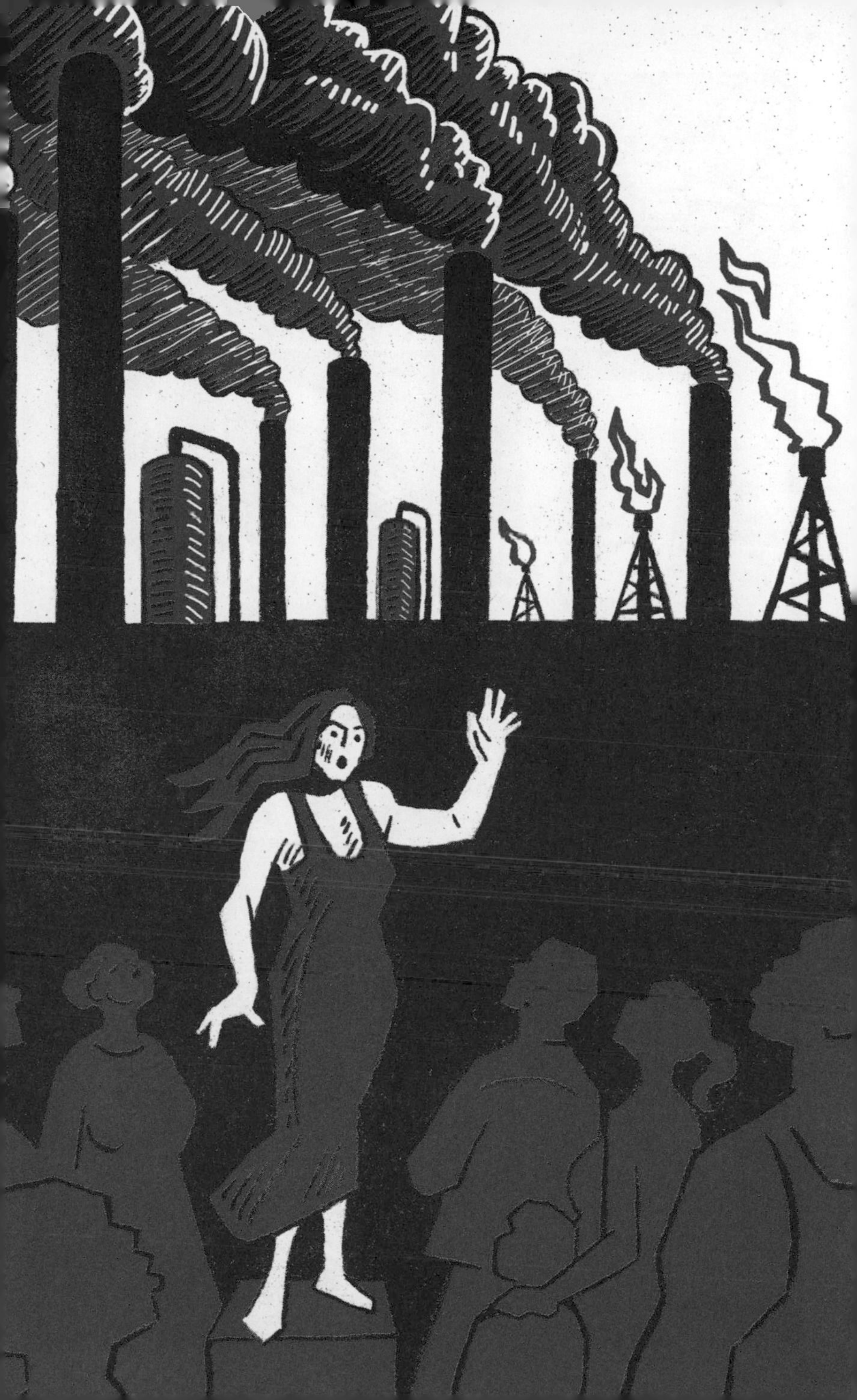

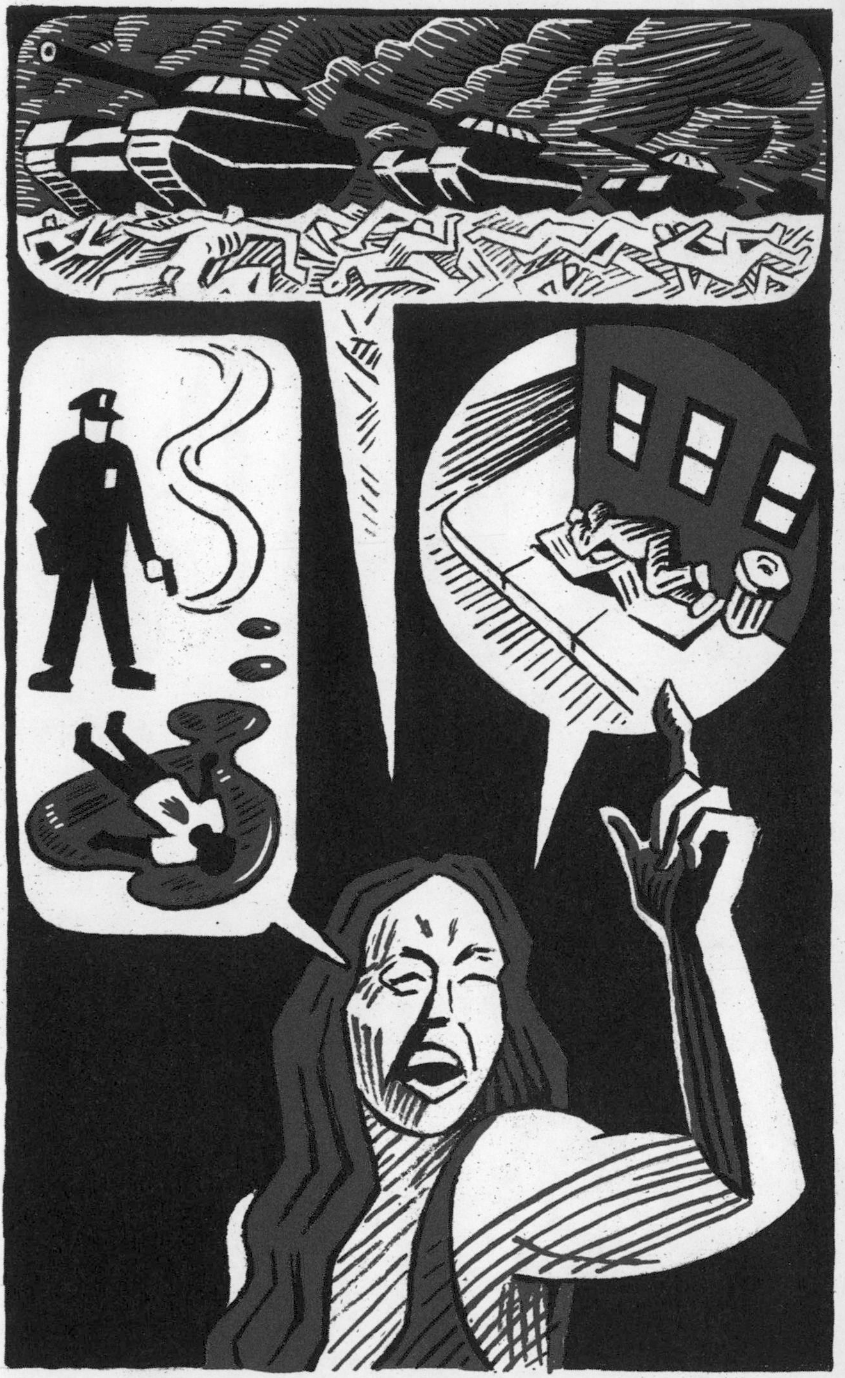

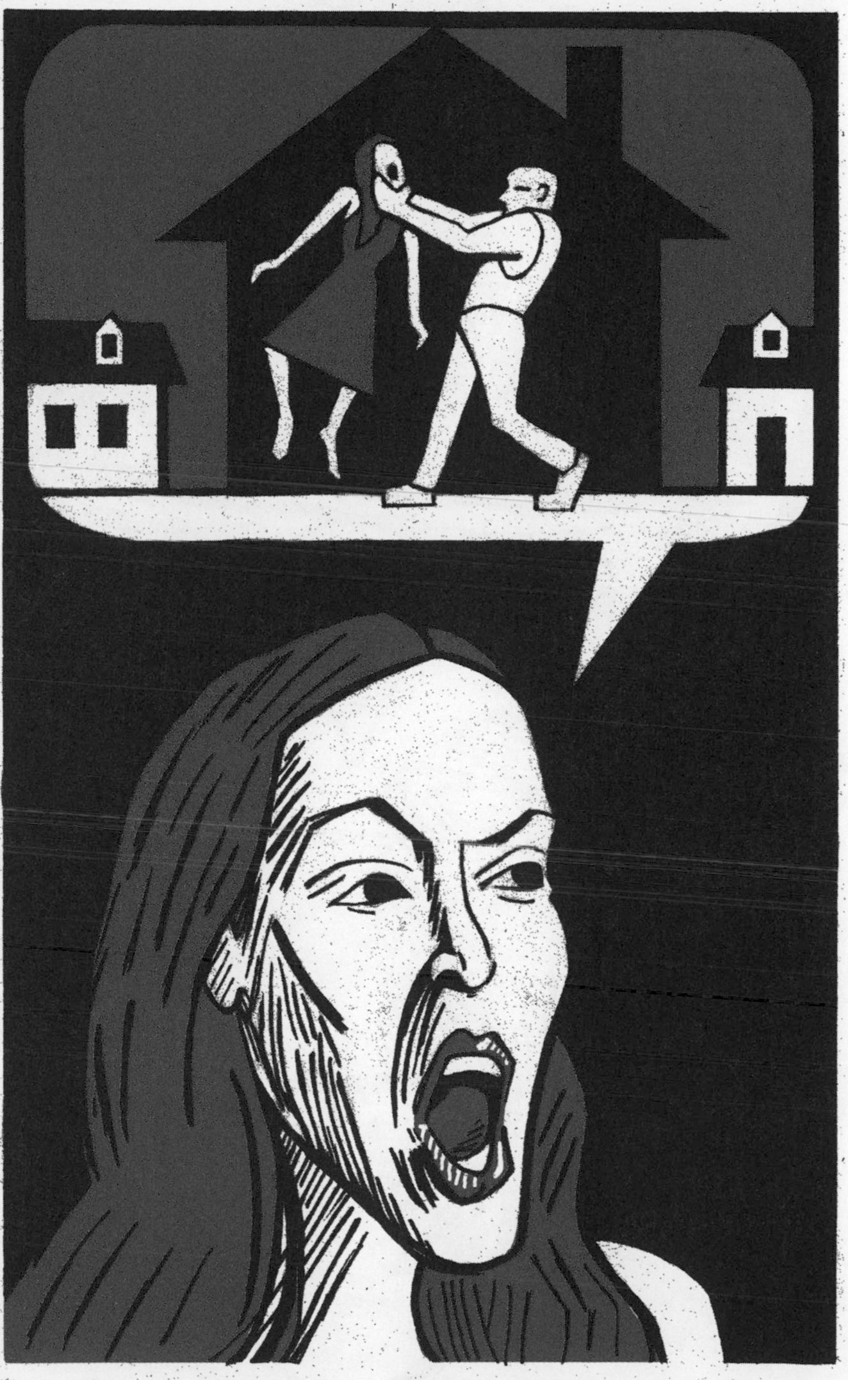

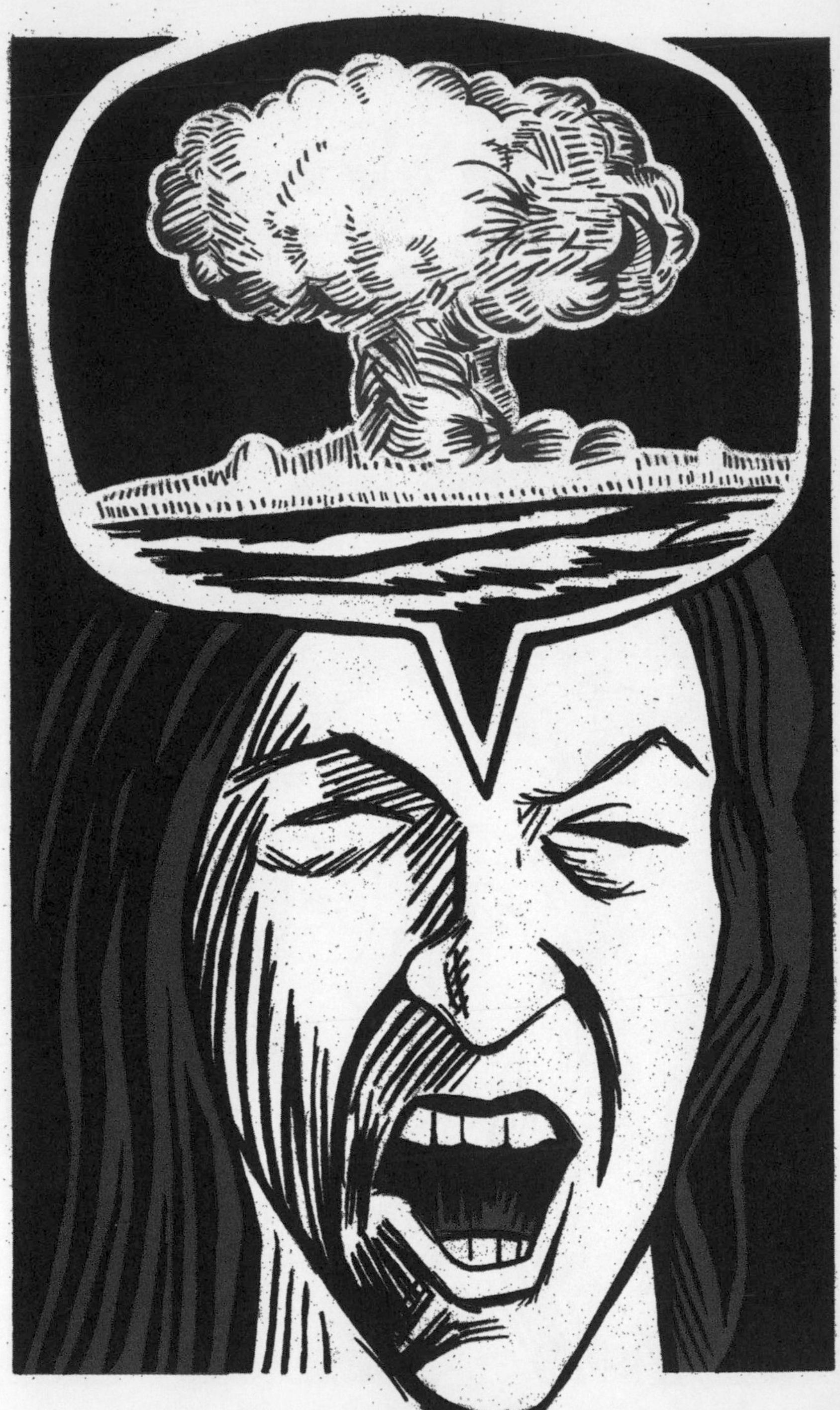

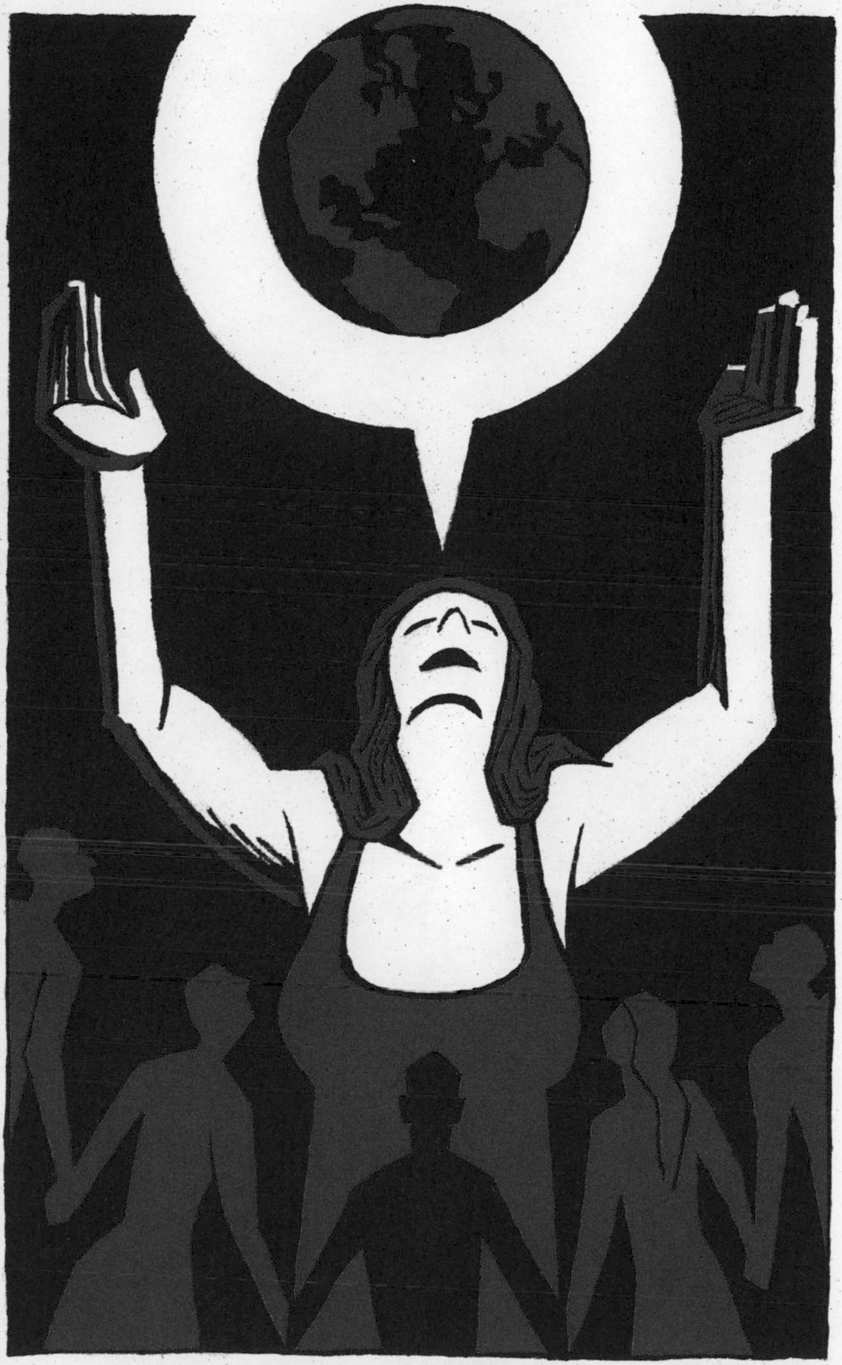

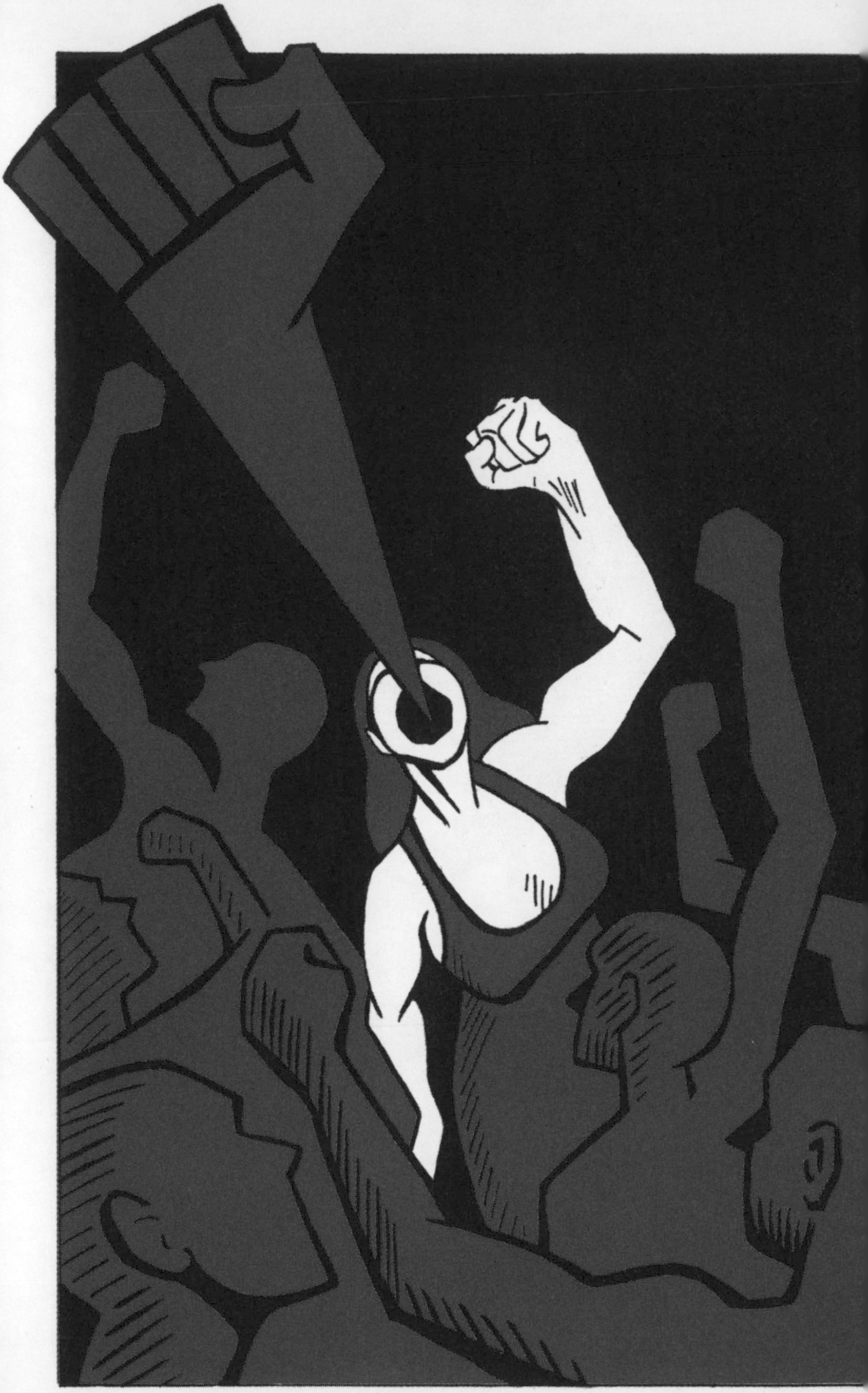

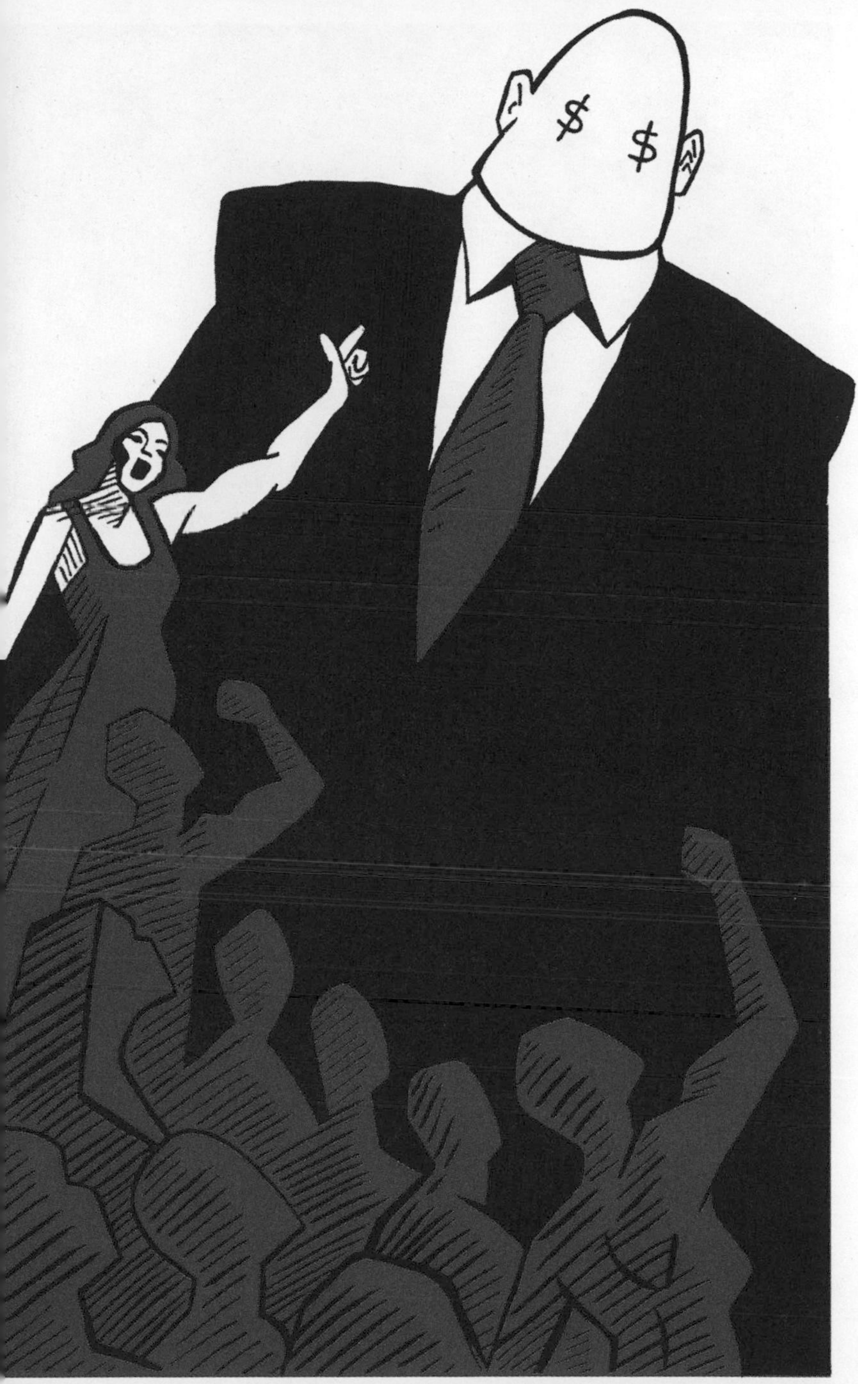

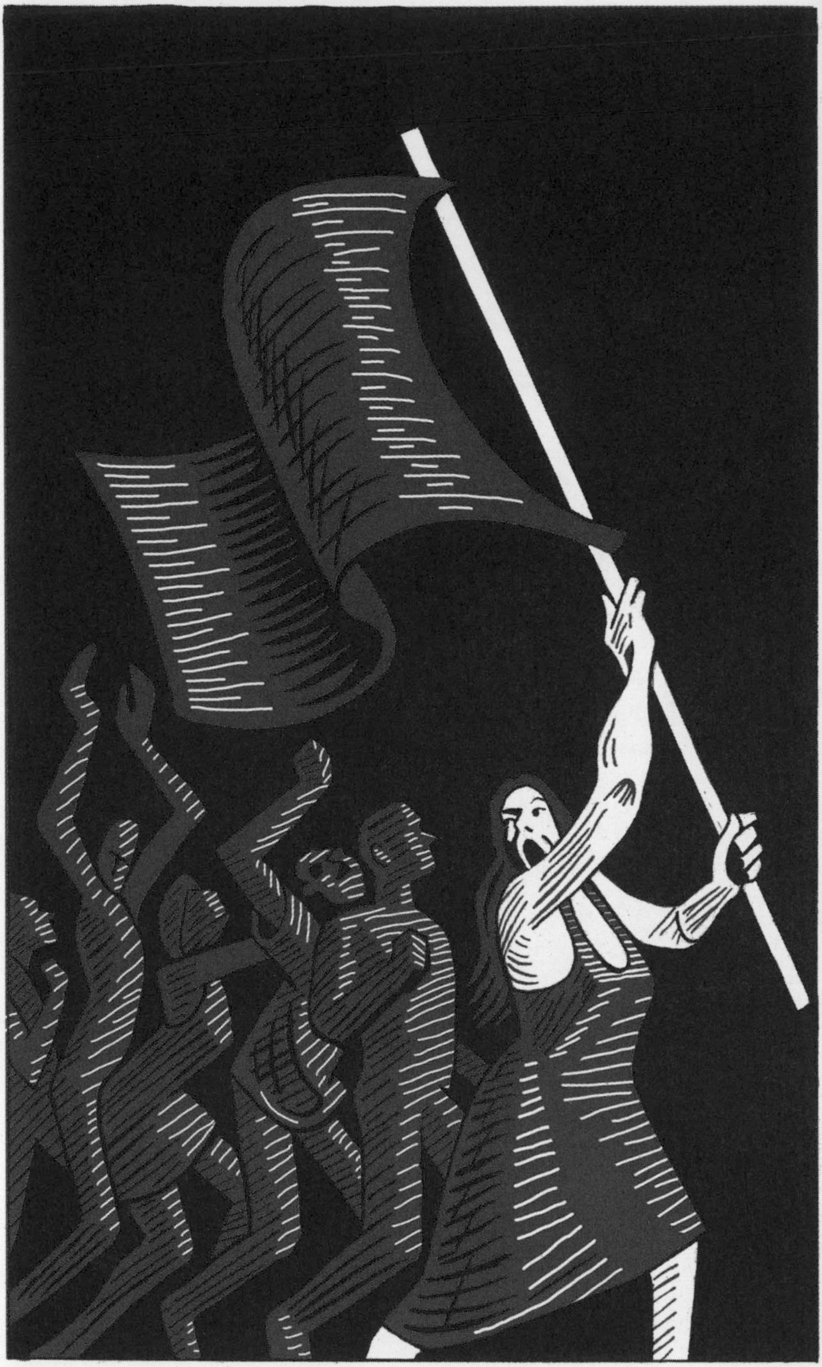

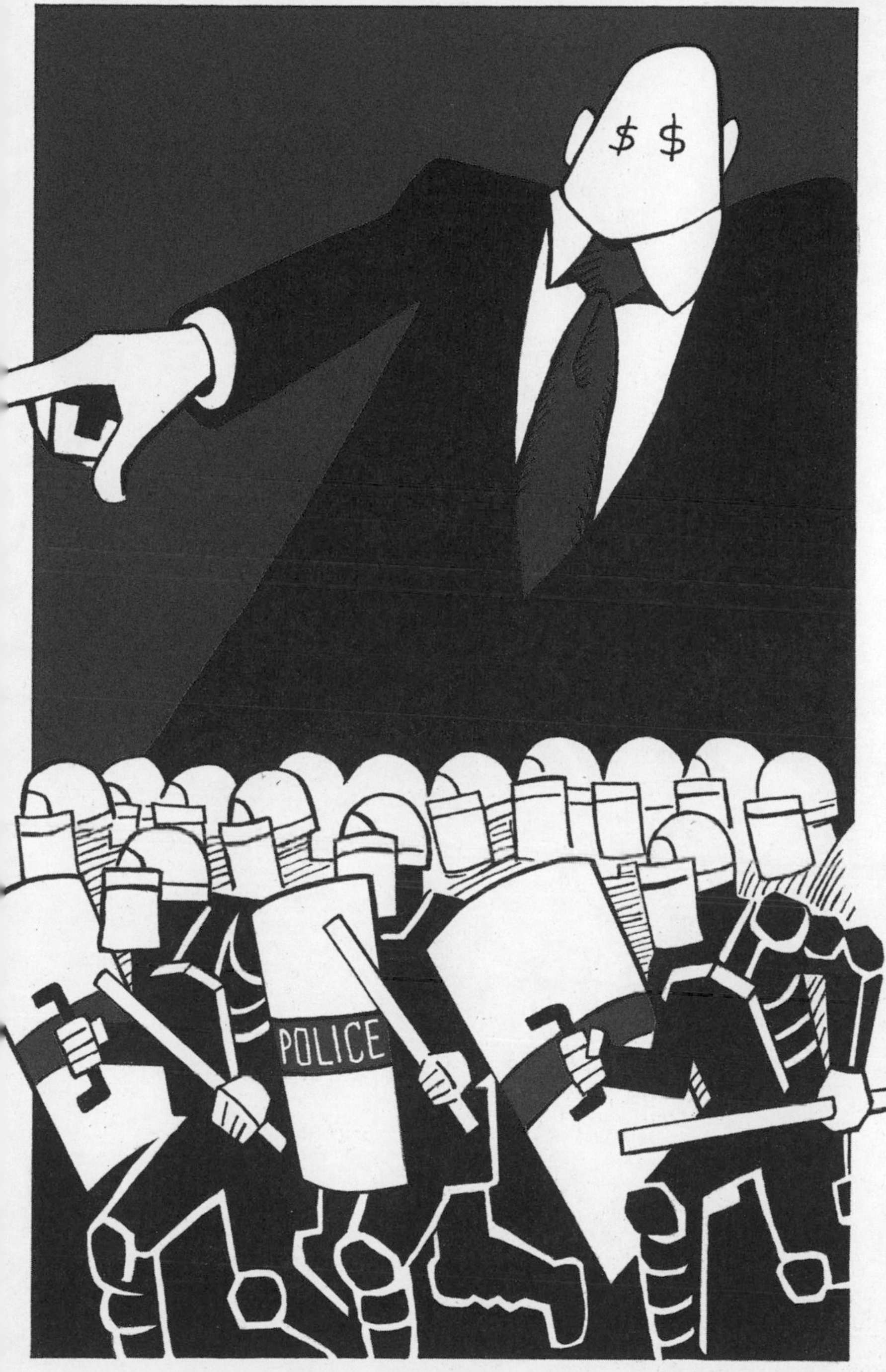

$ $
POLICE

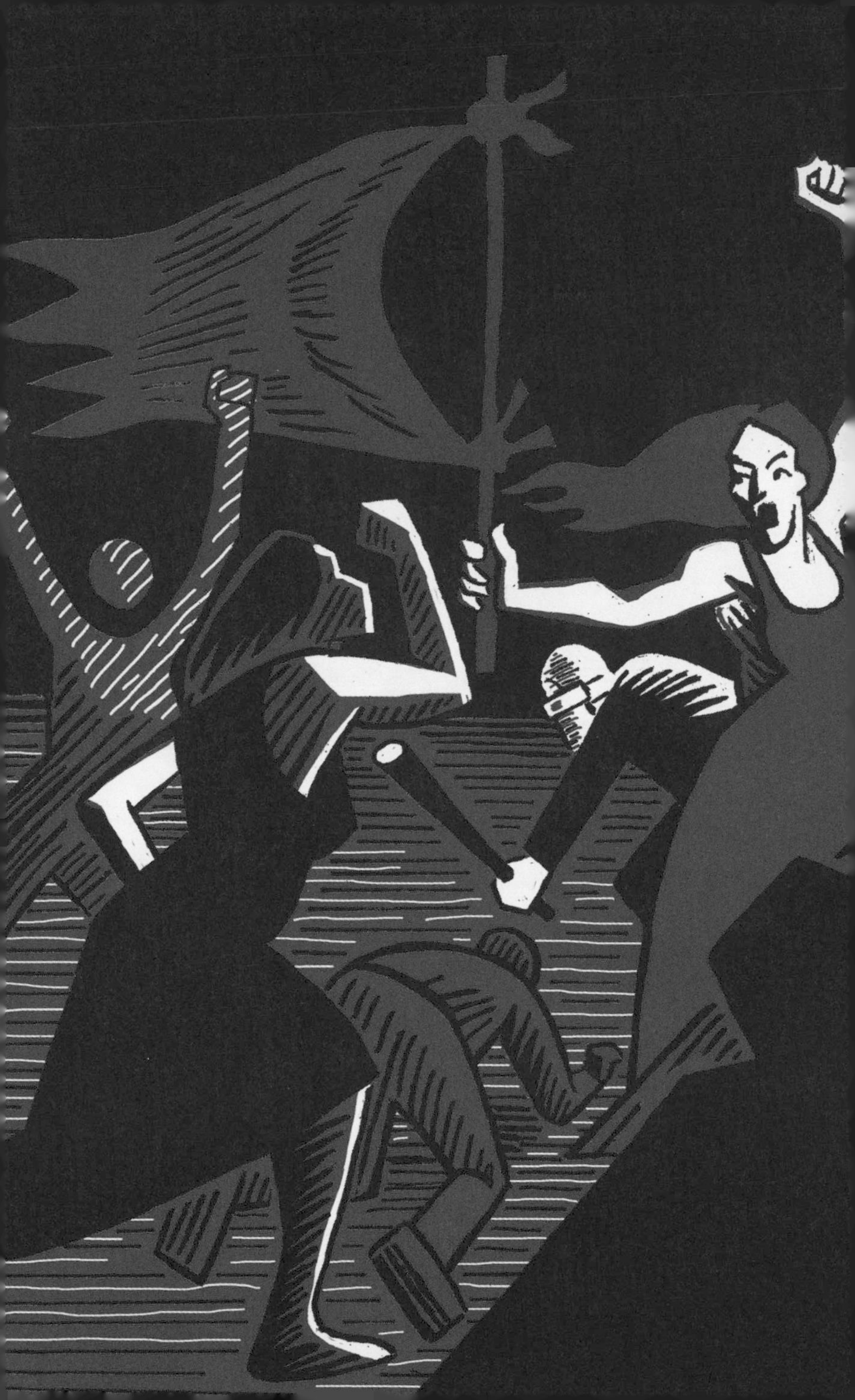

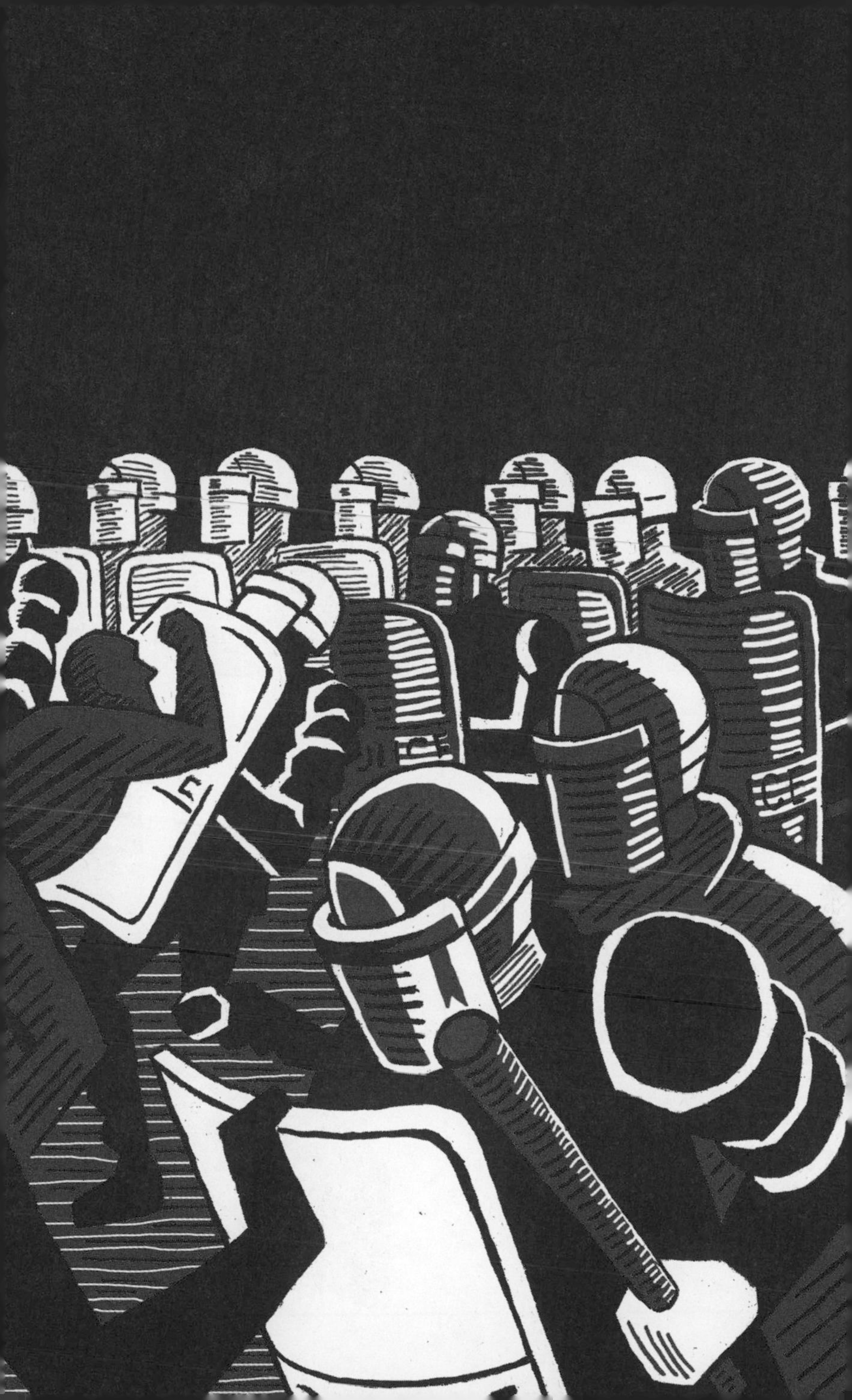

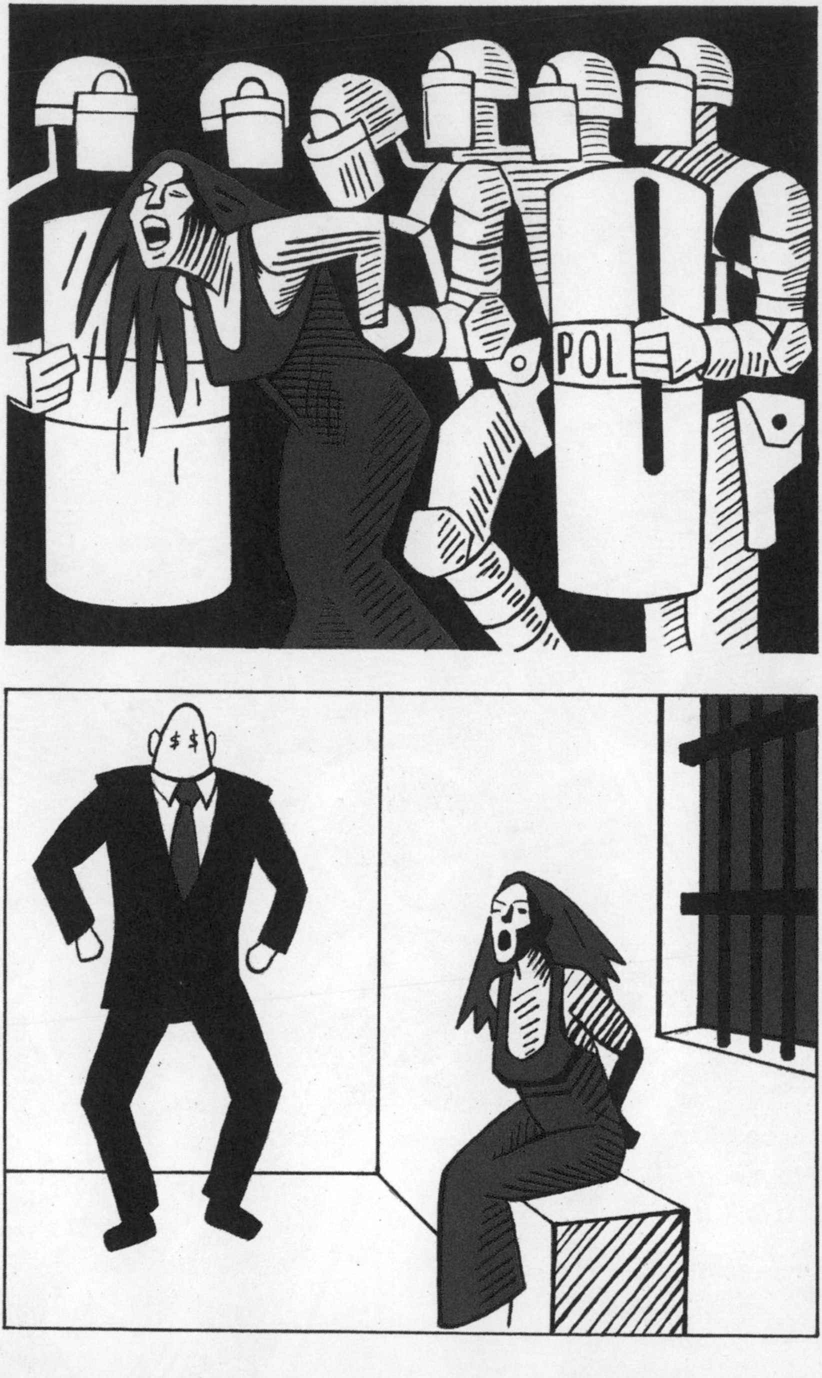
POL

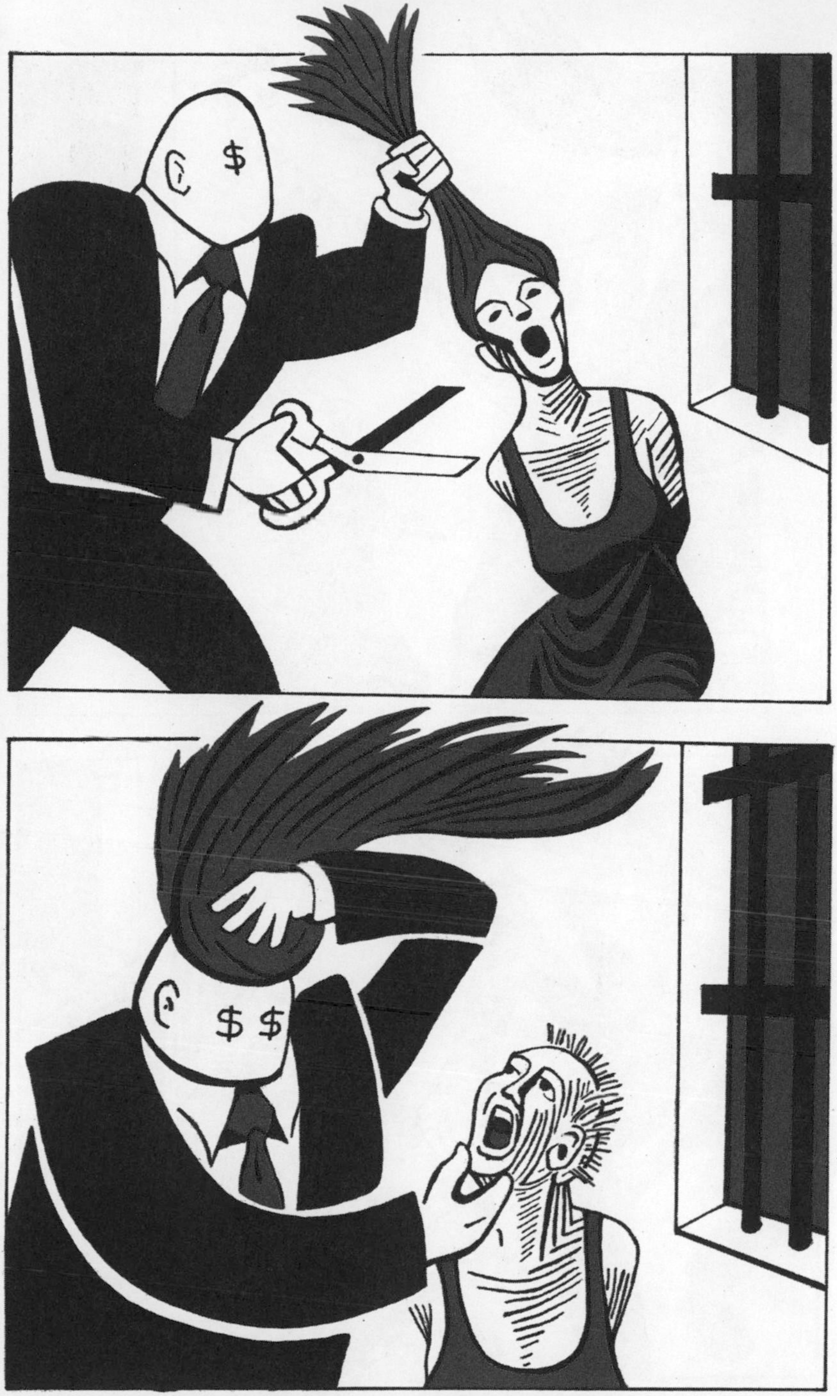

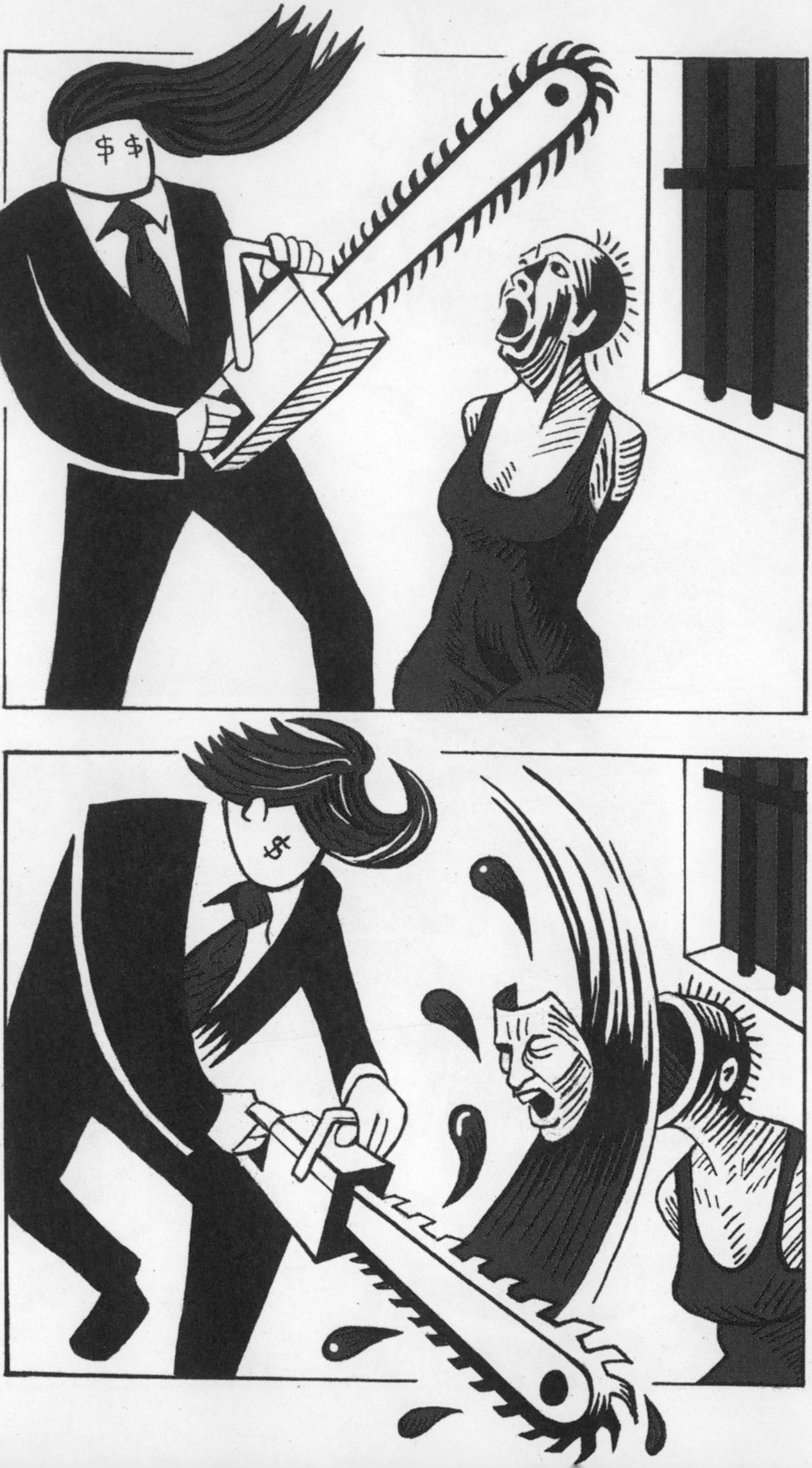

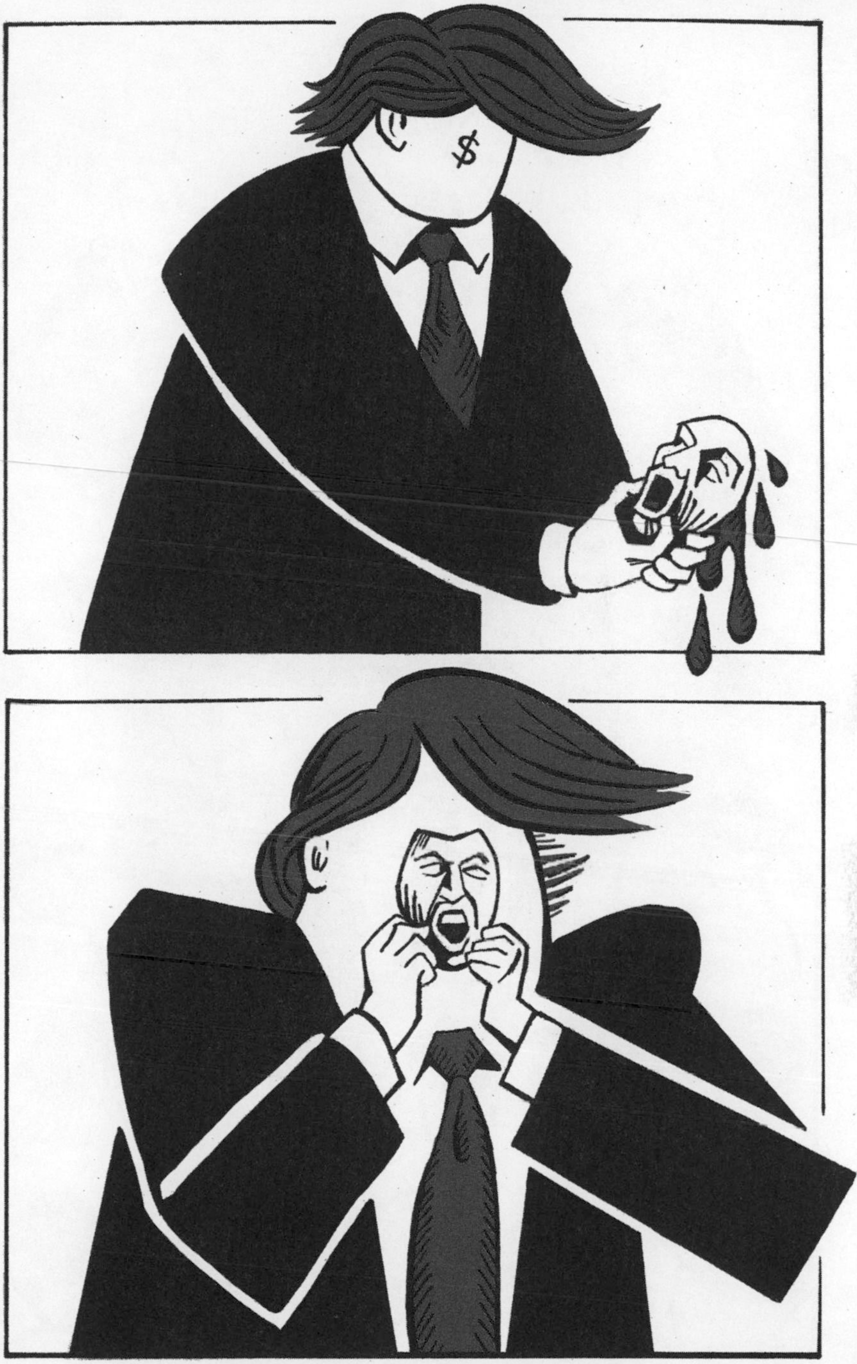

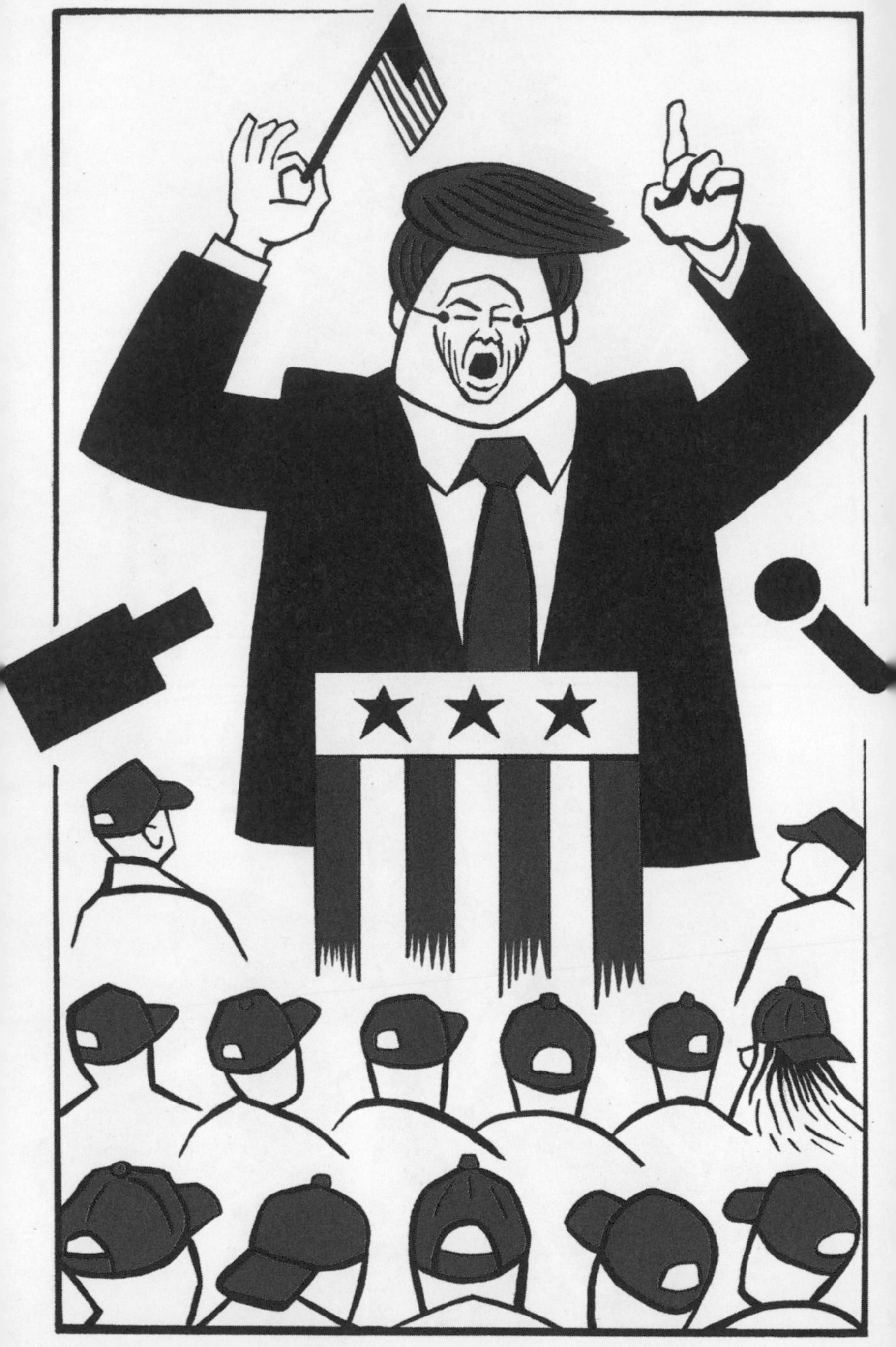

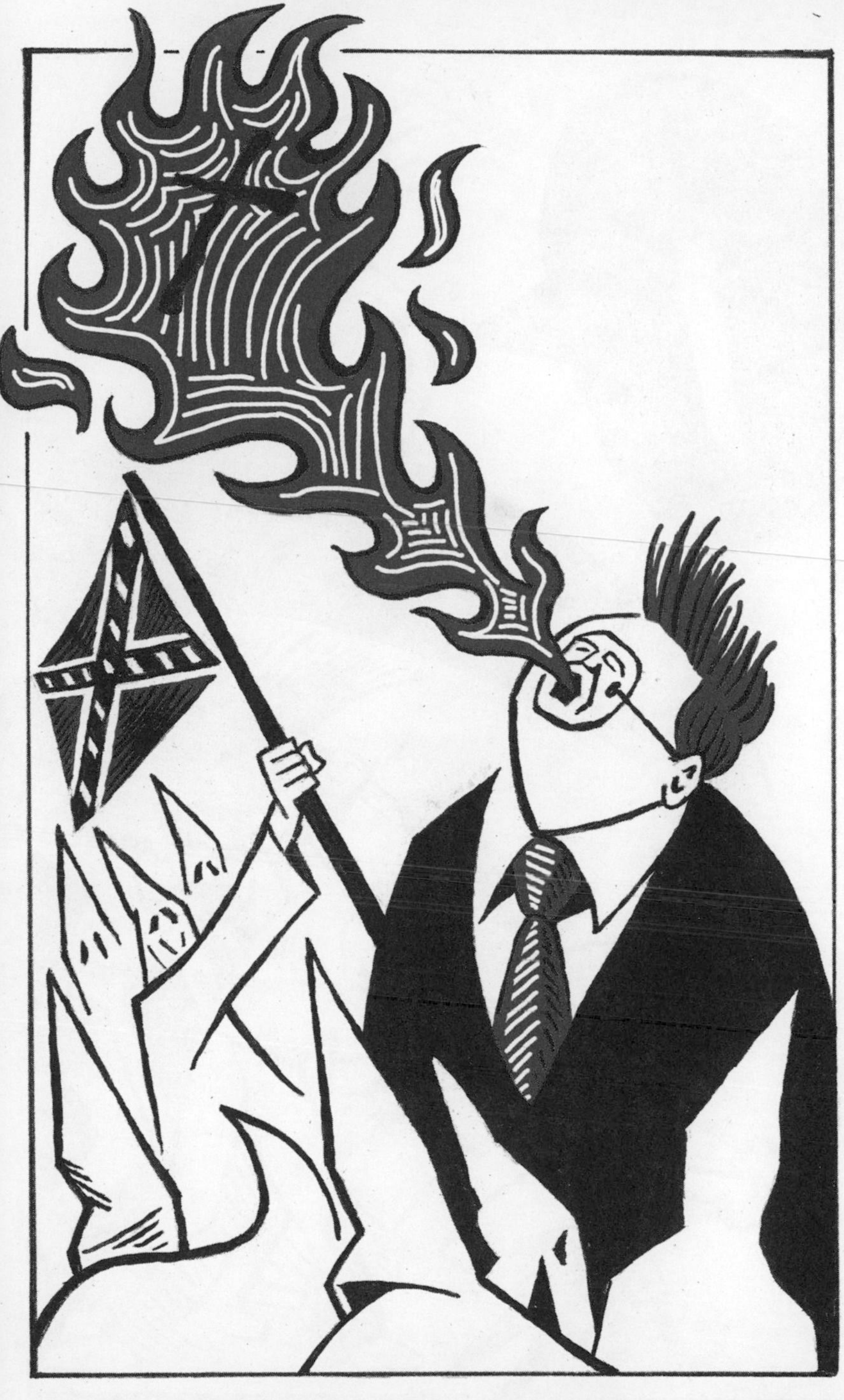

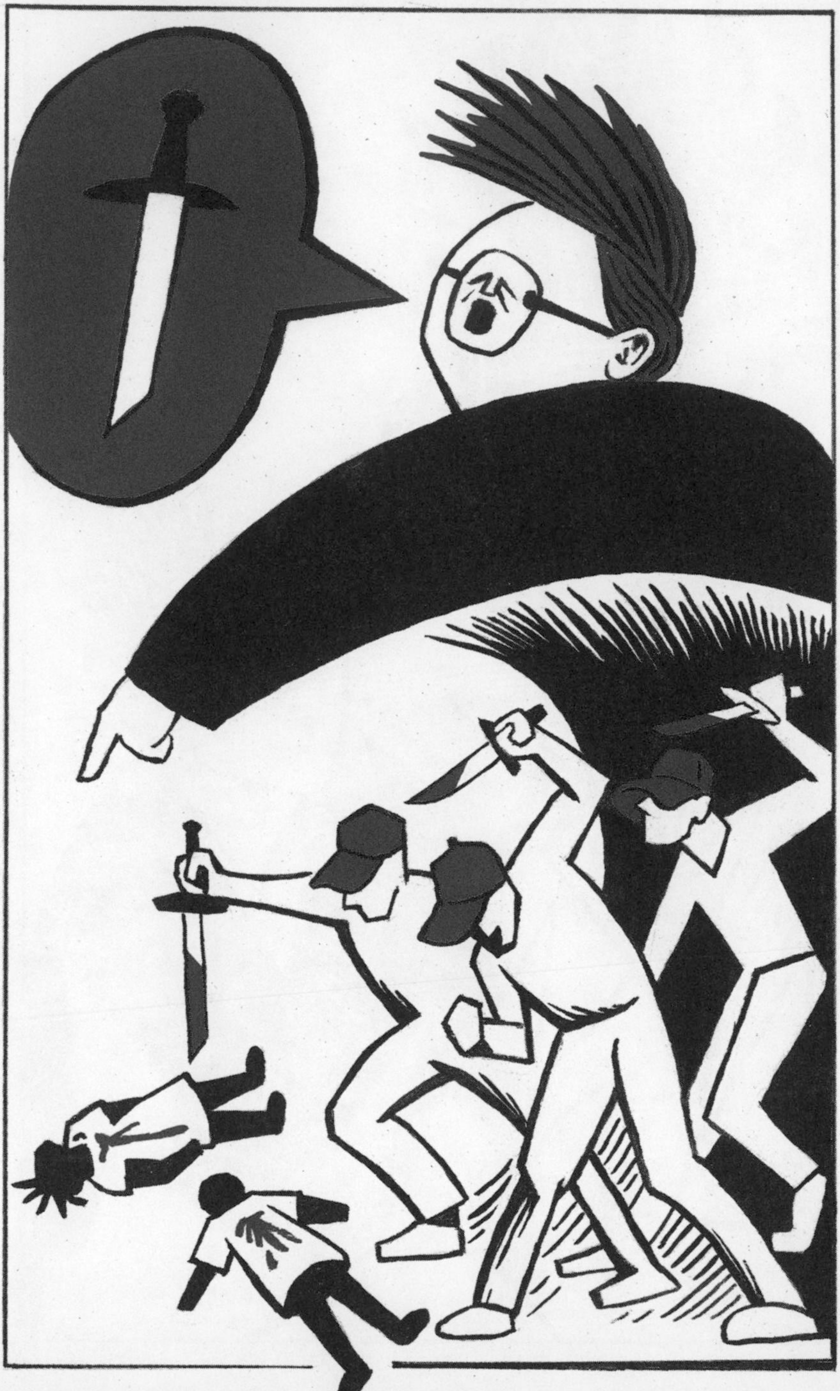

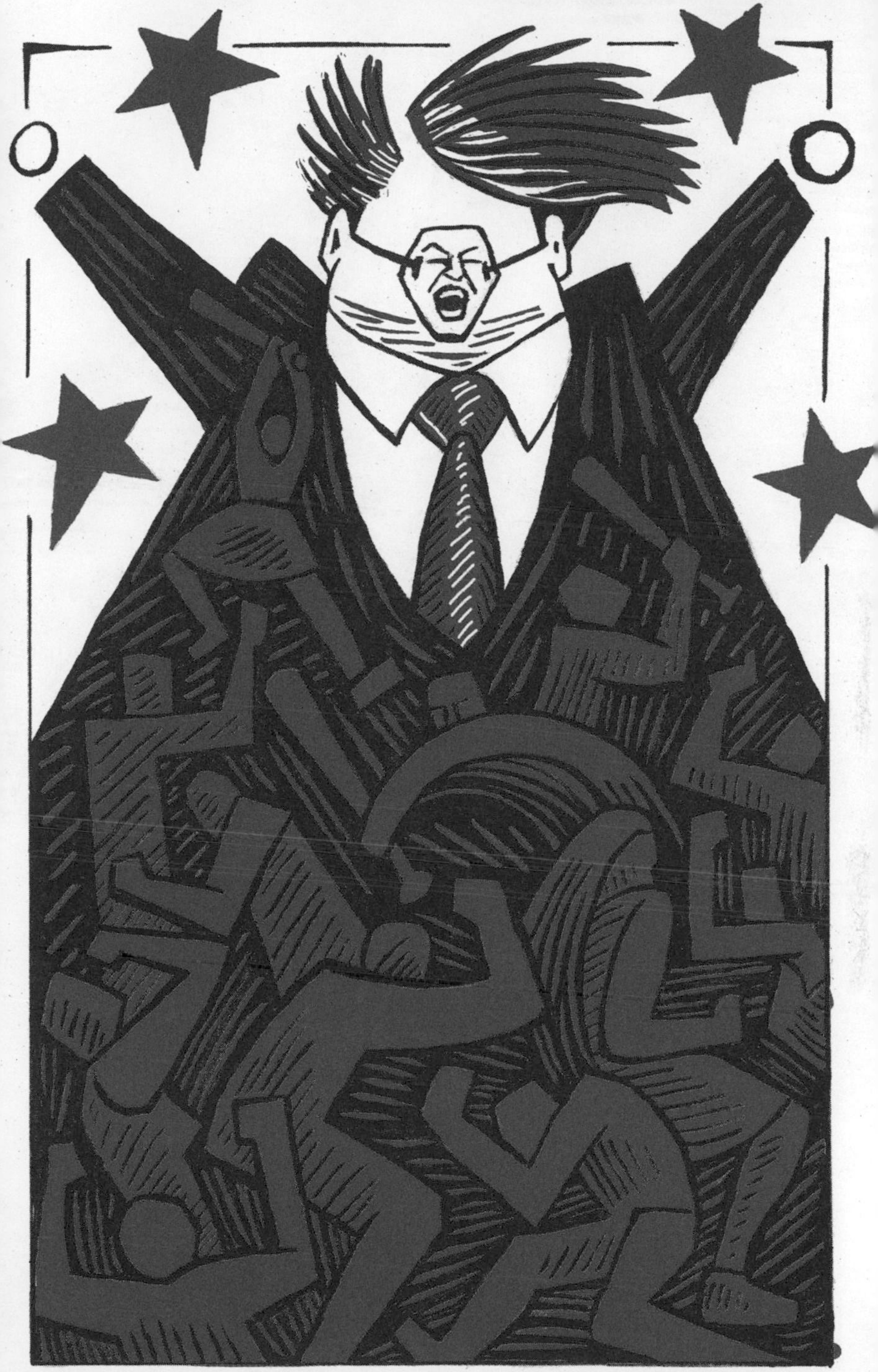

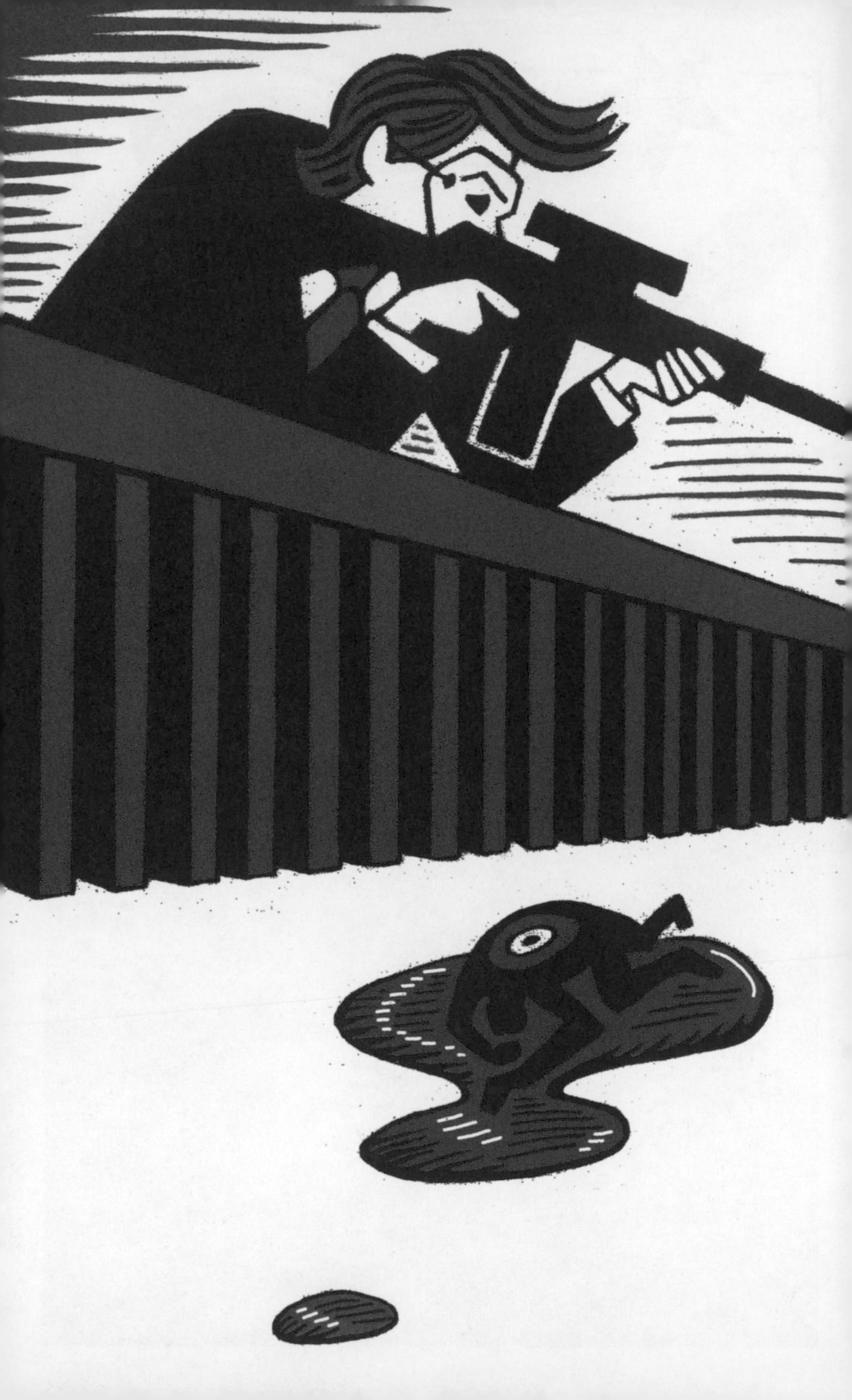

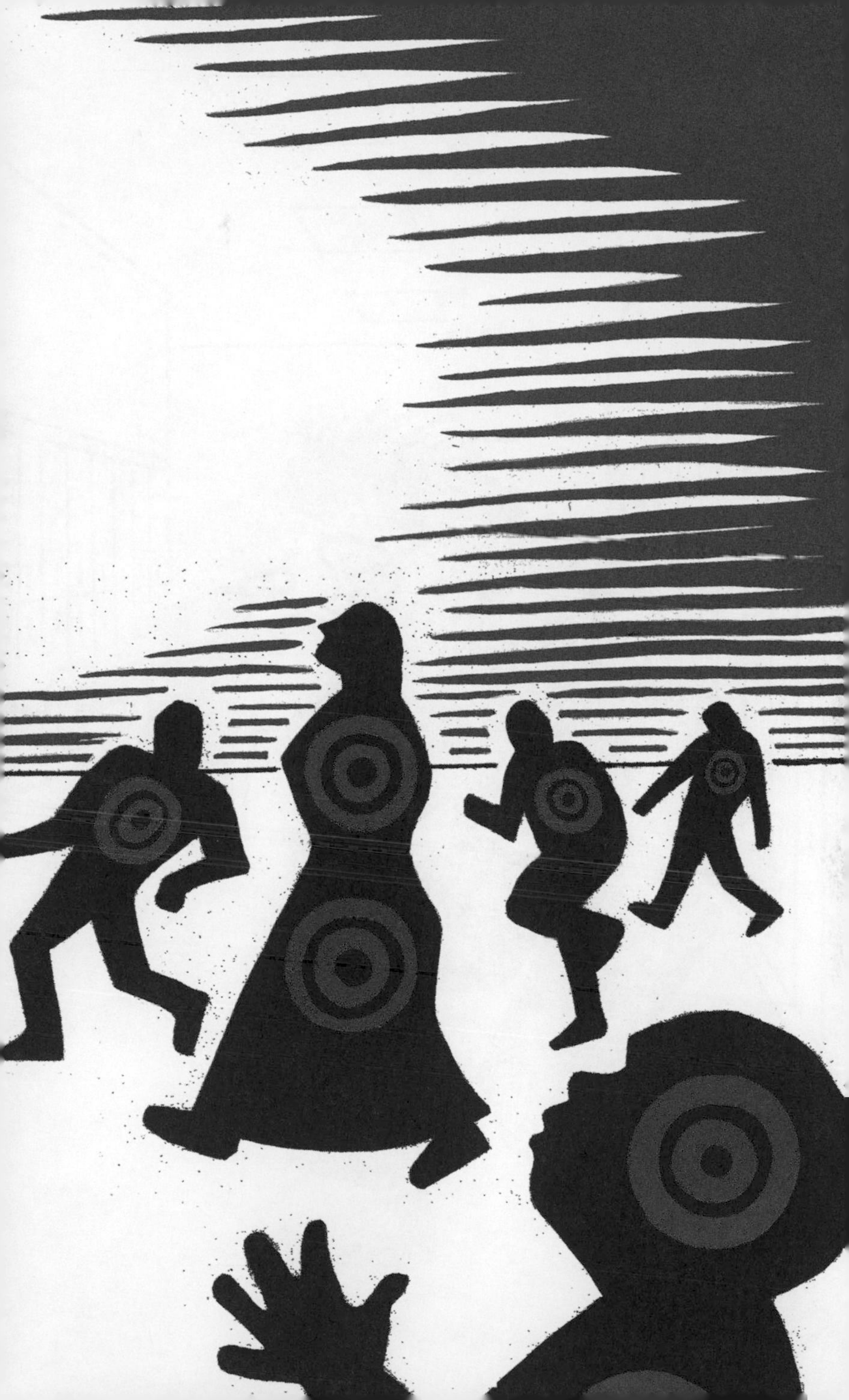

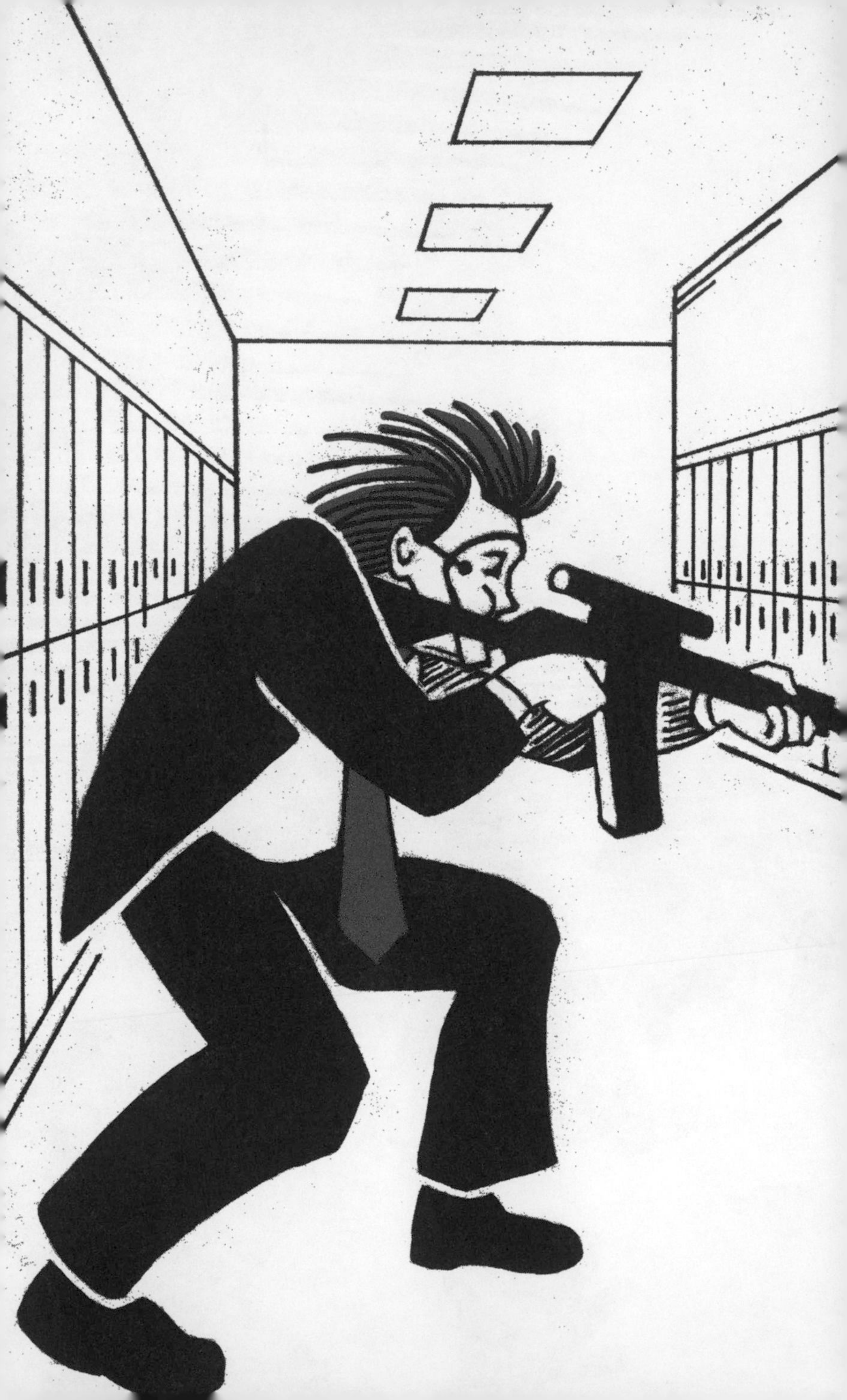

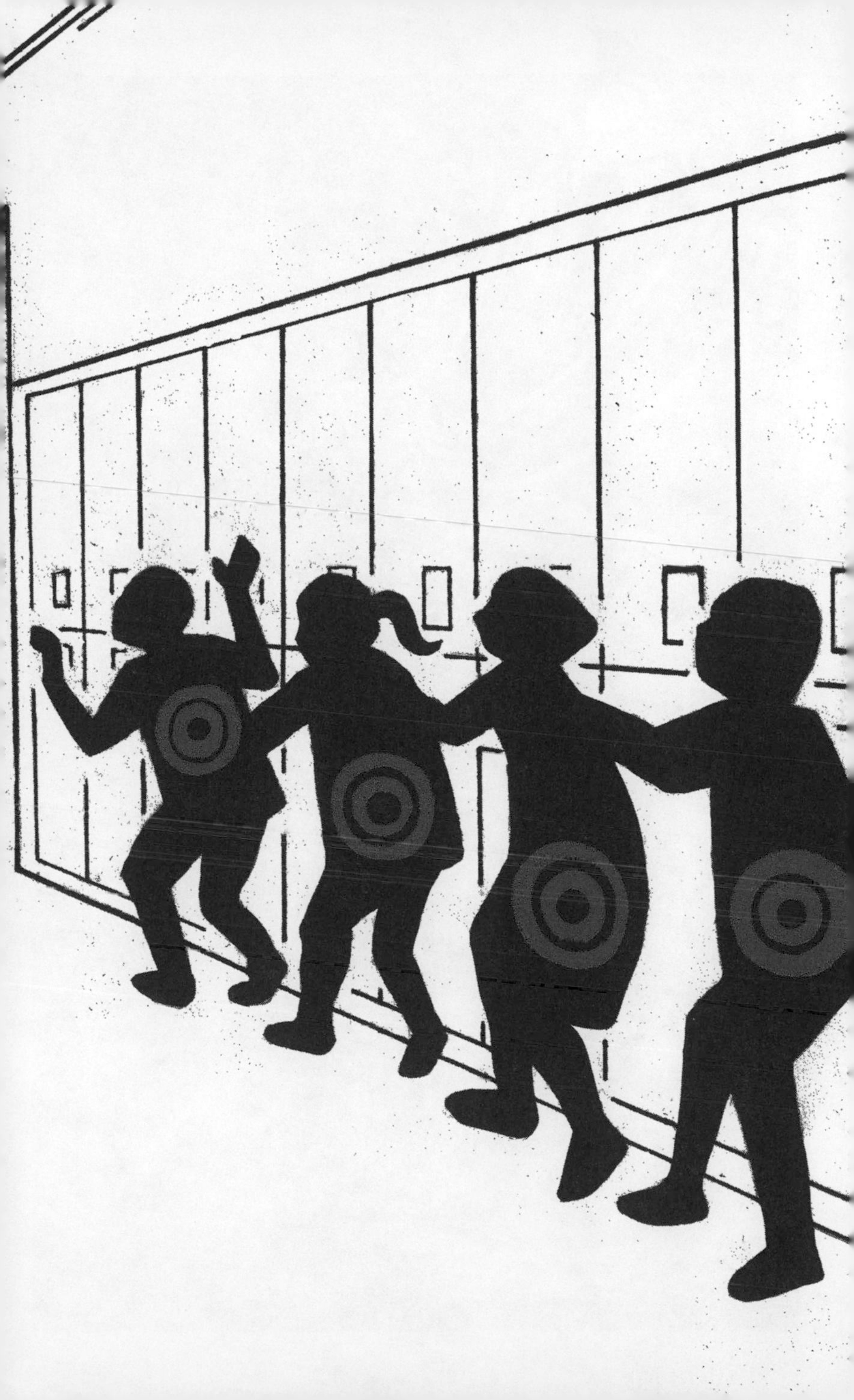

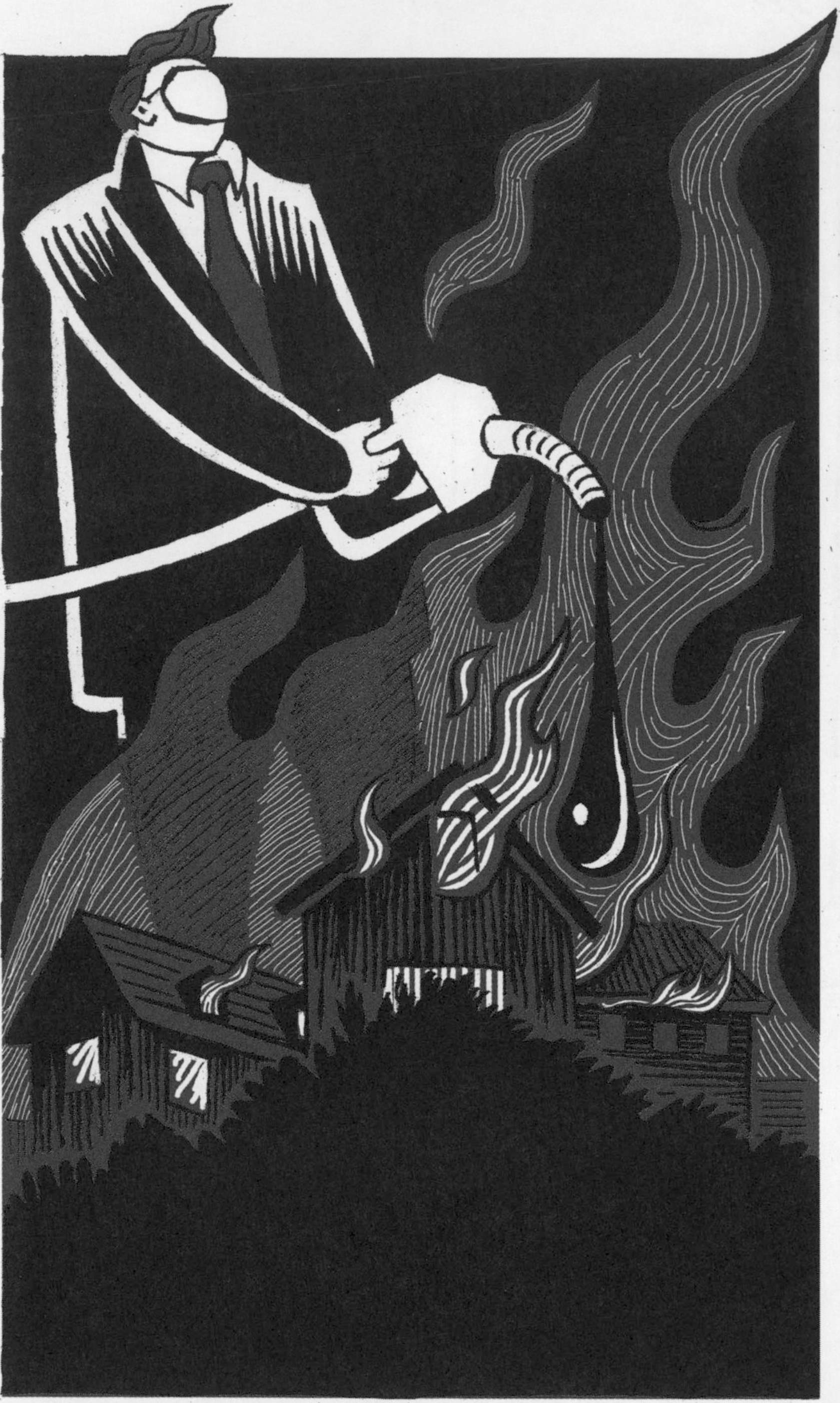

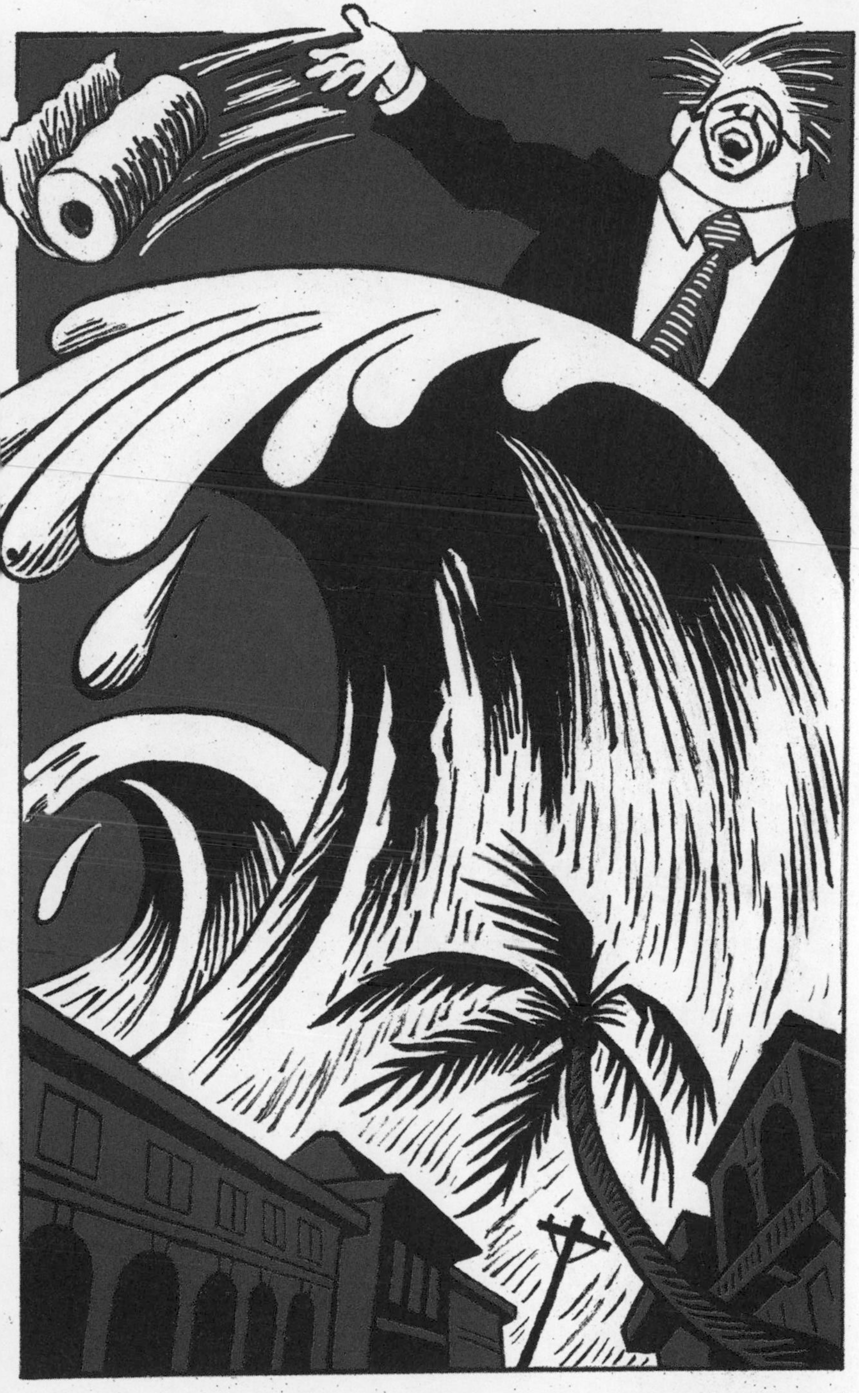

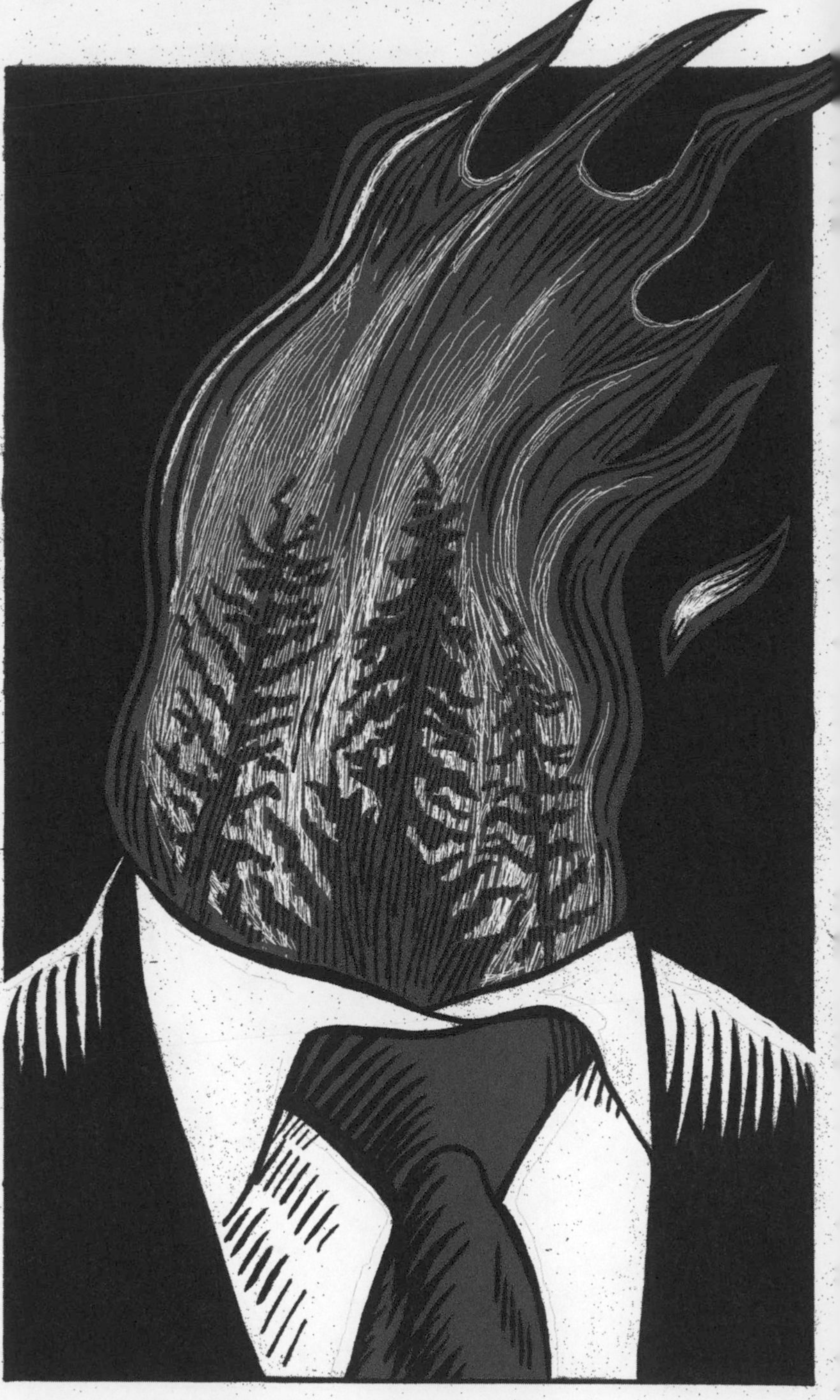

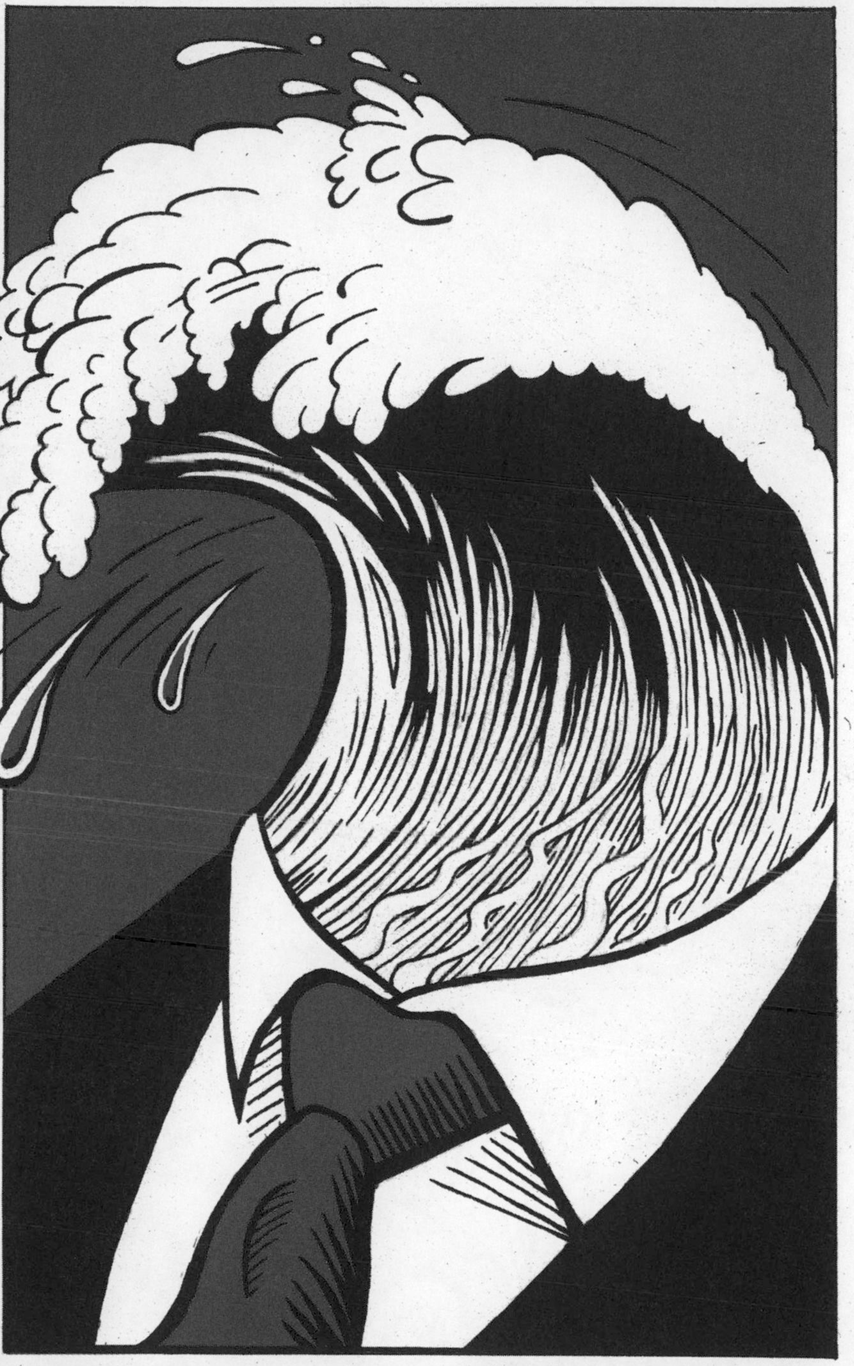

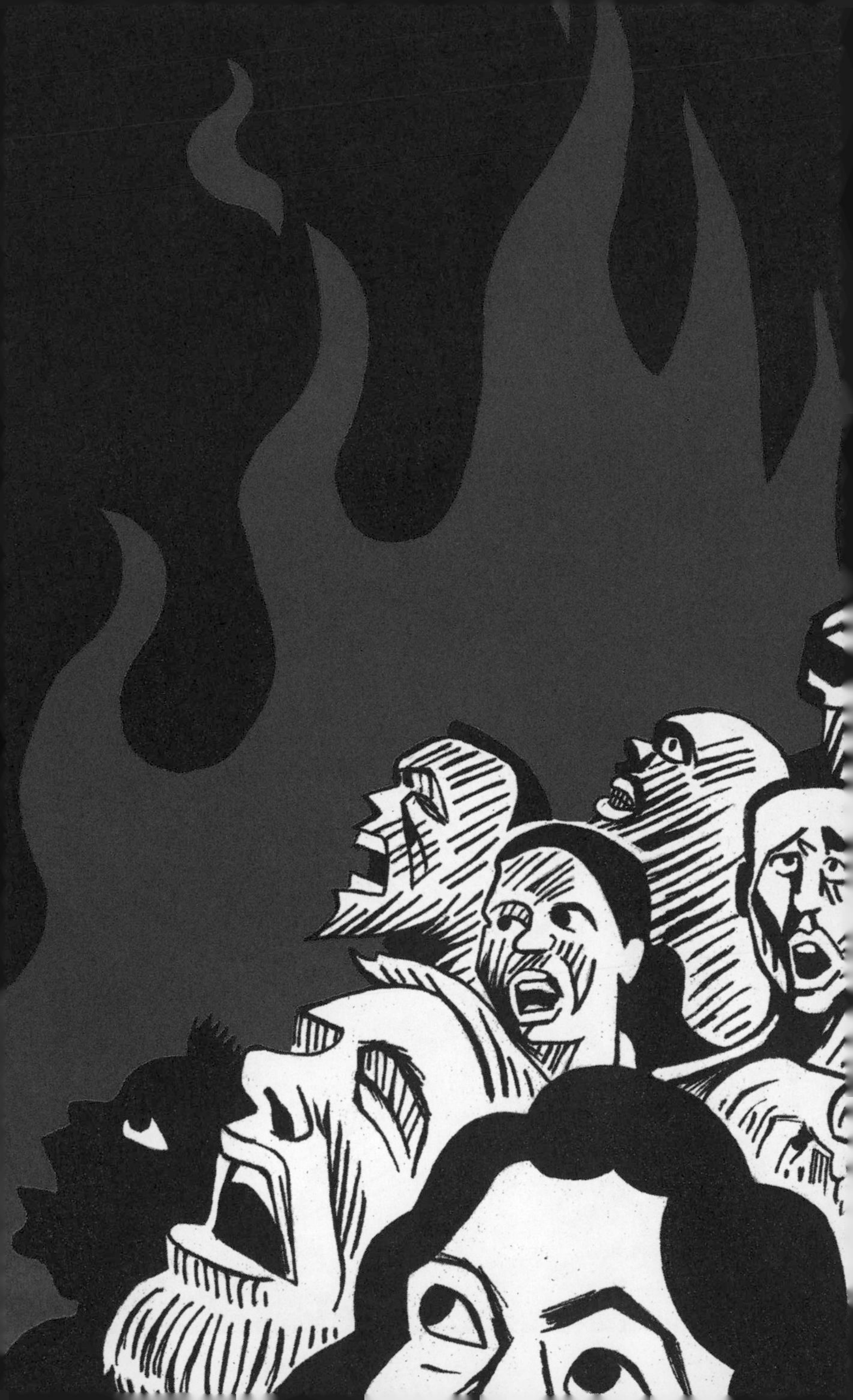

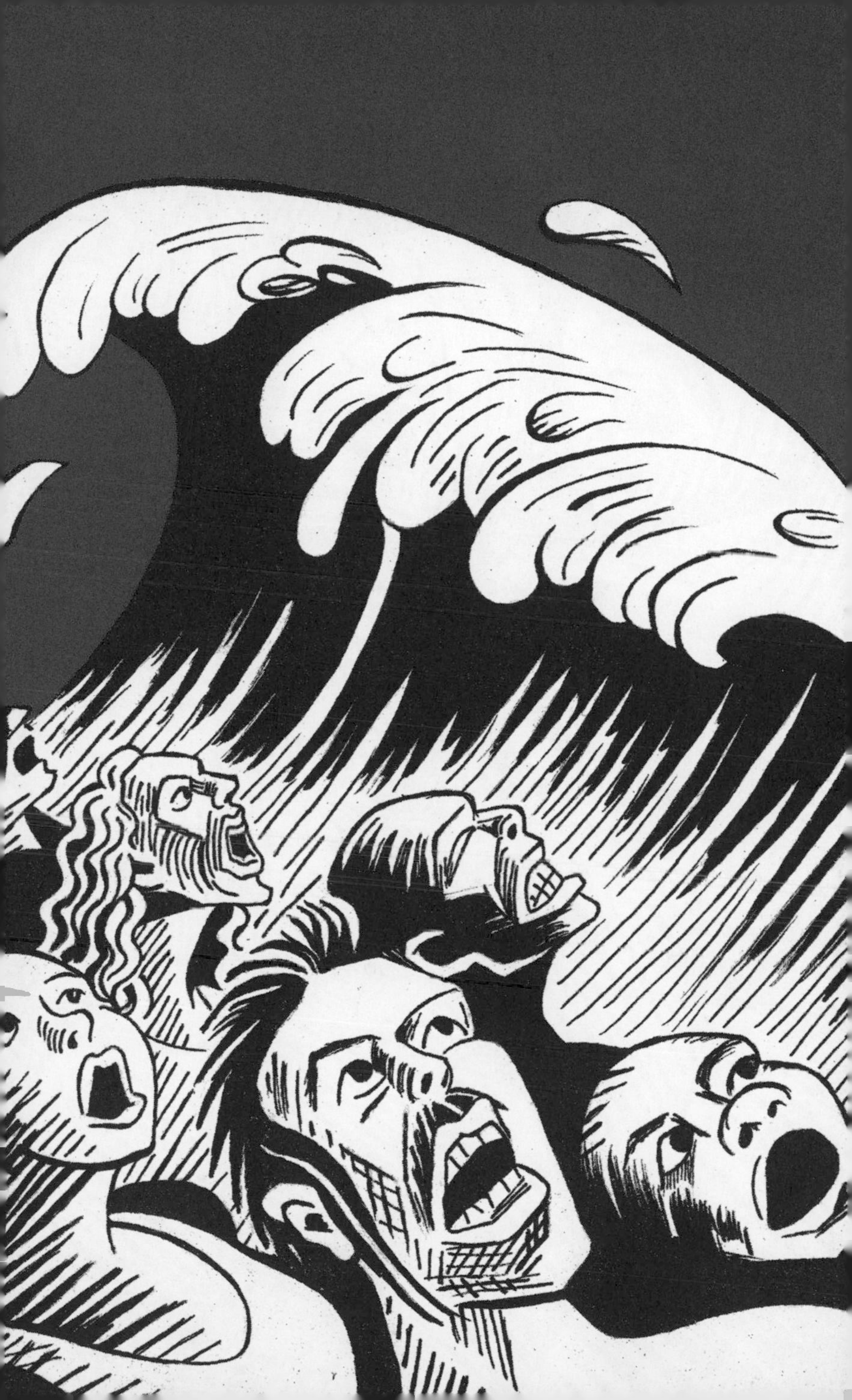

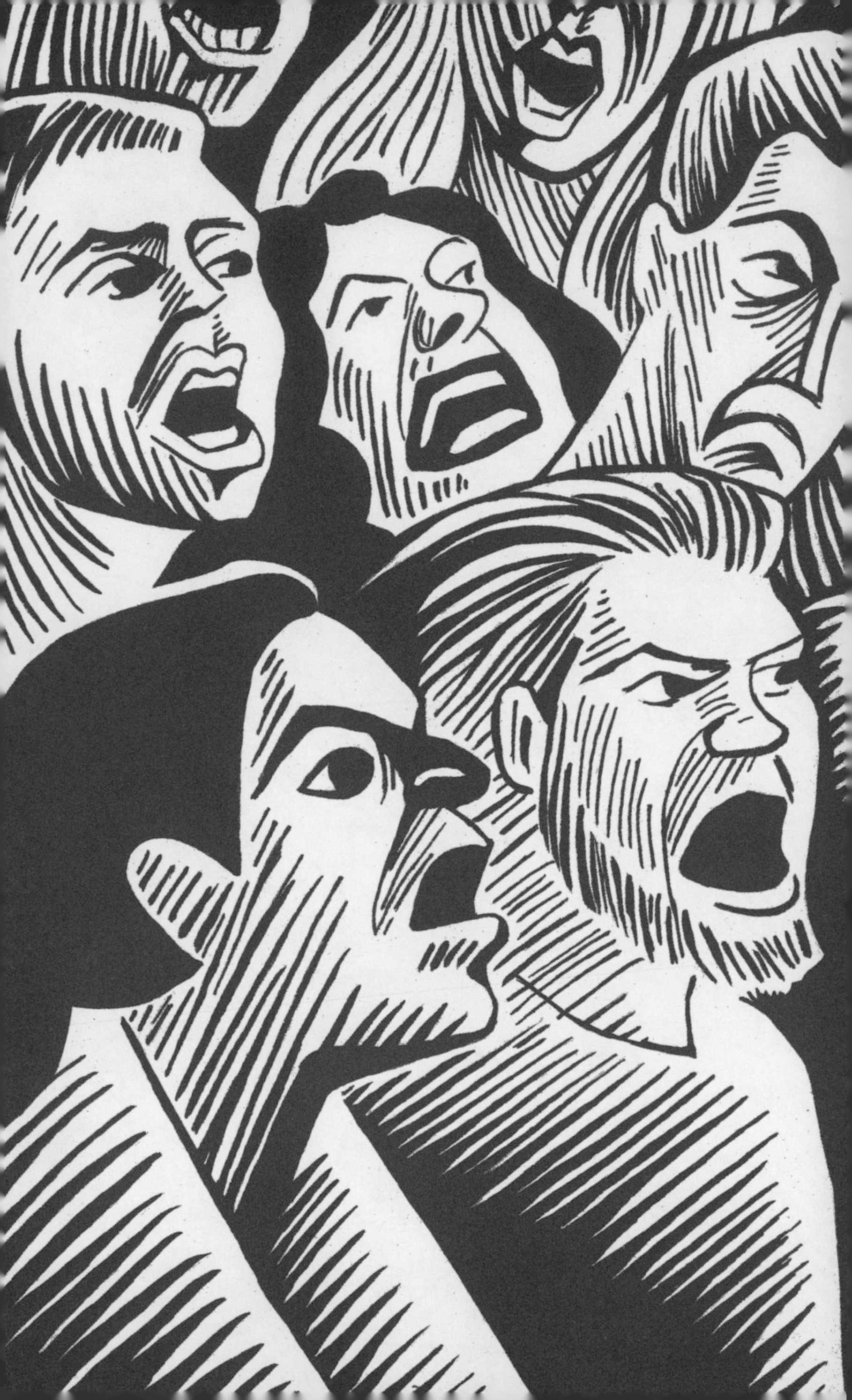

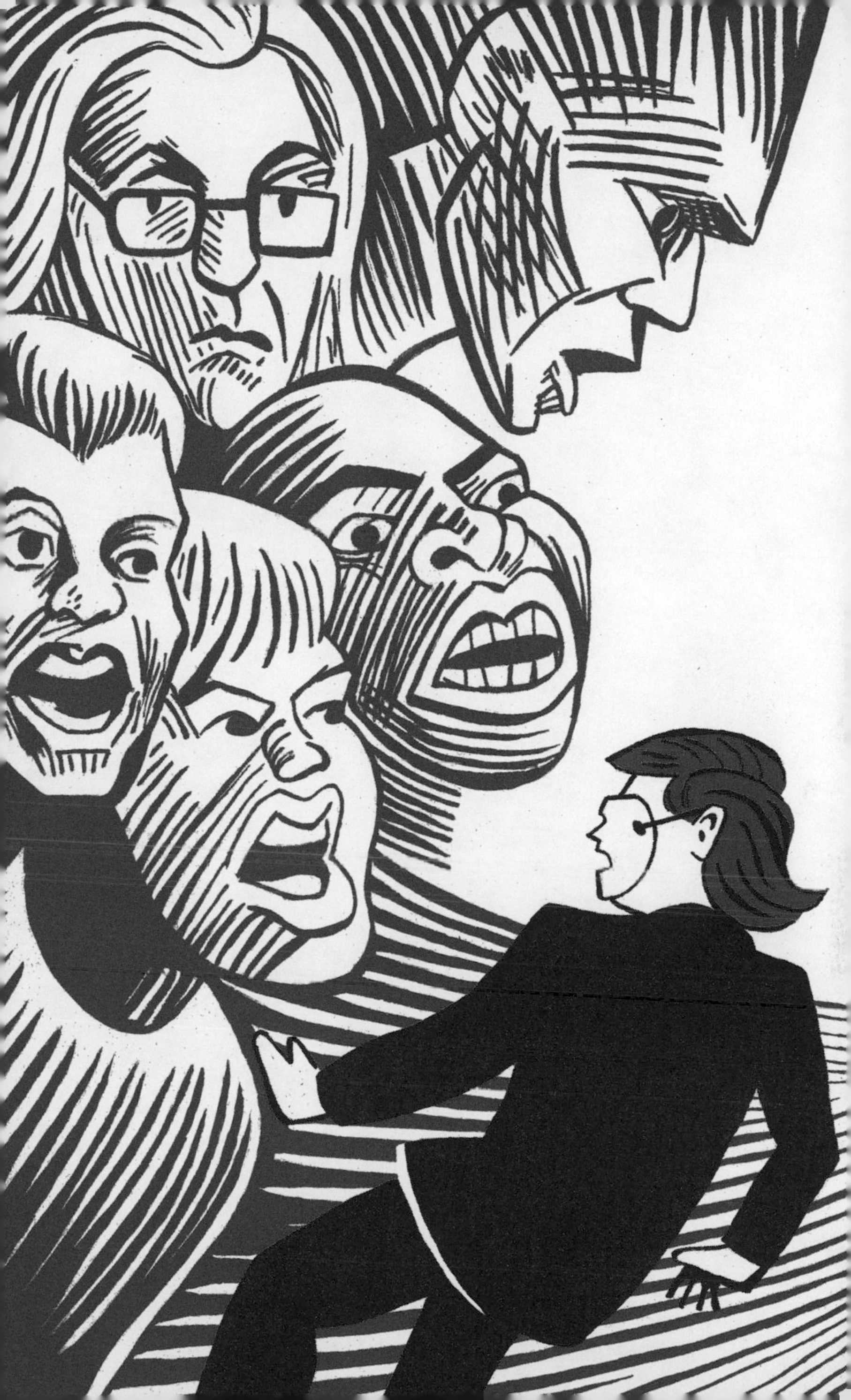

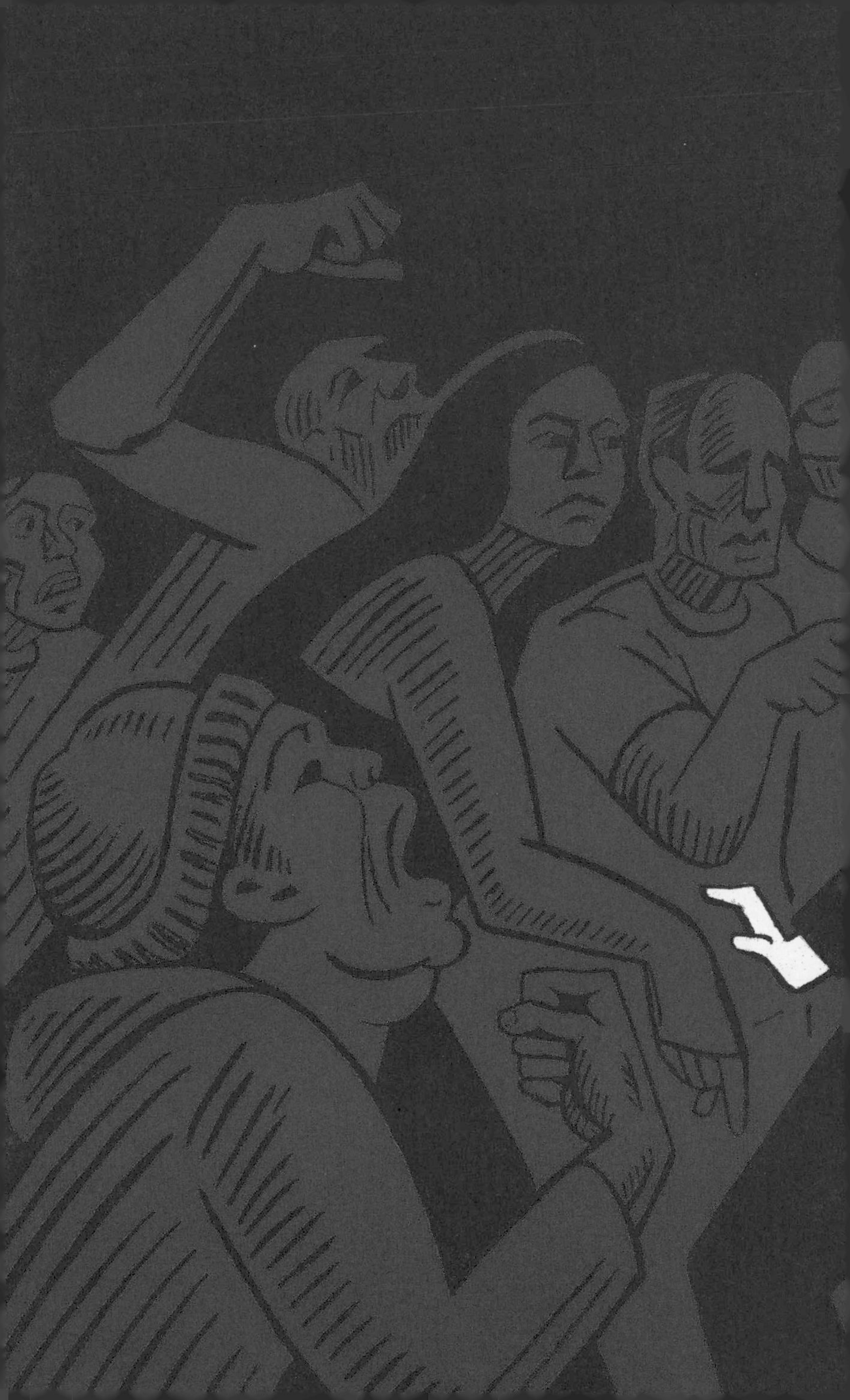

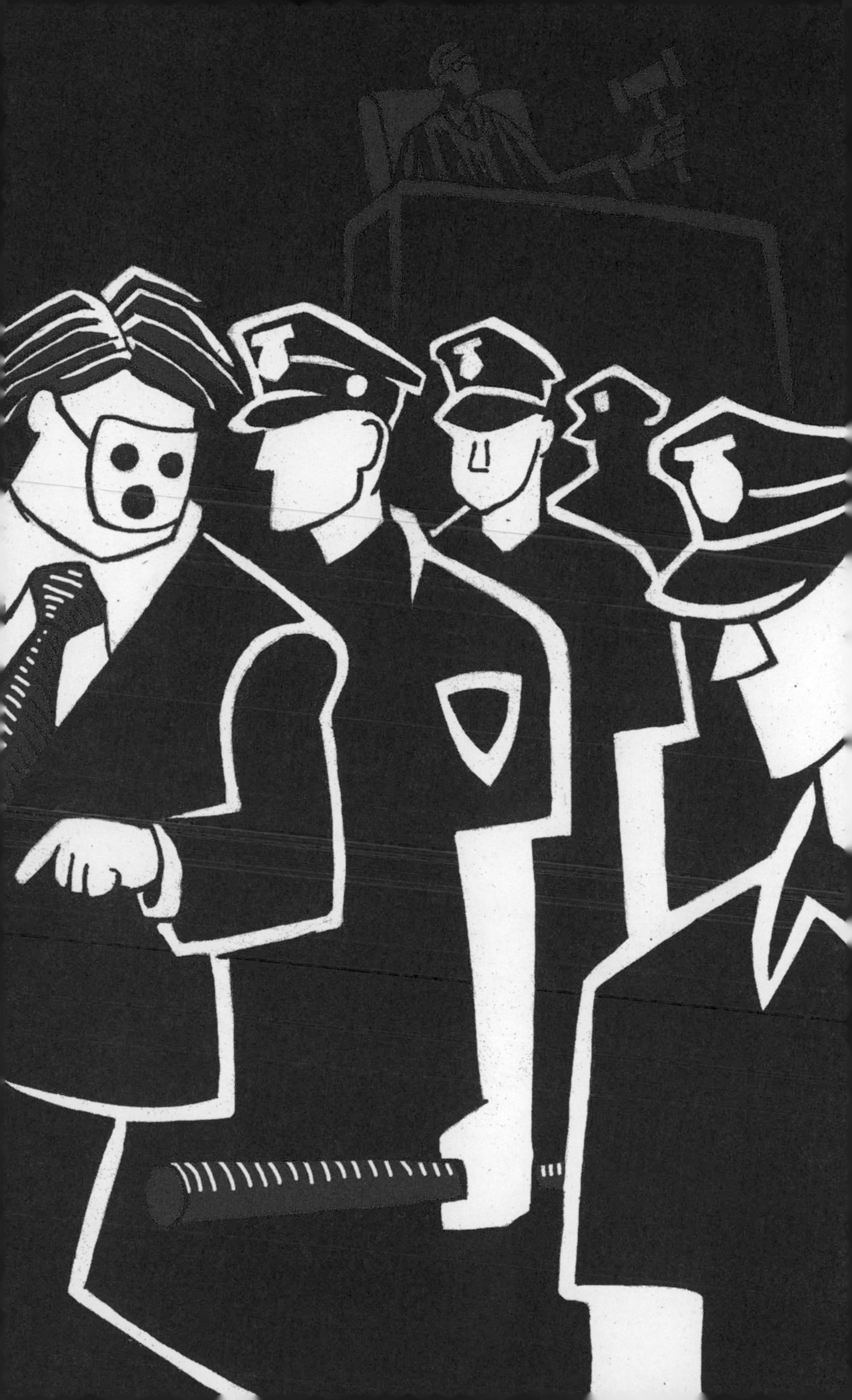

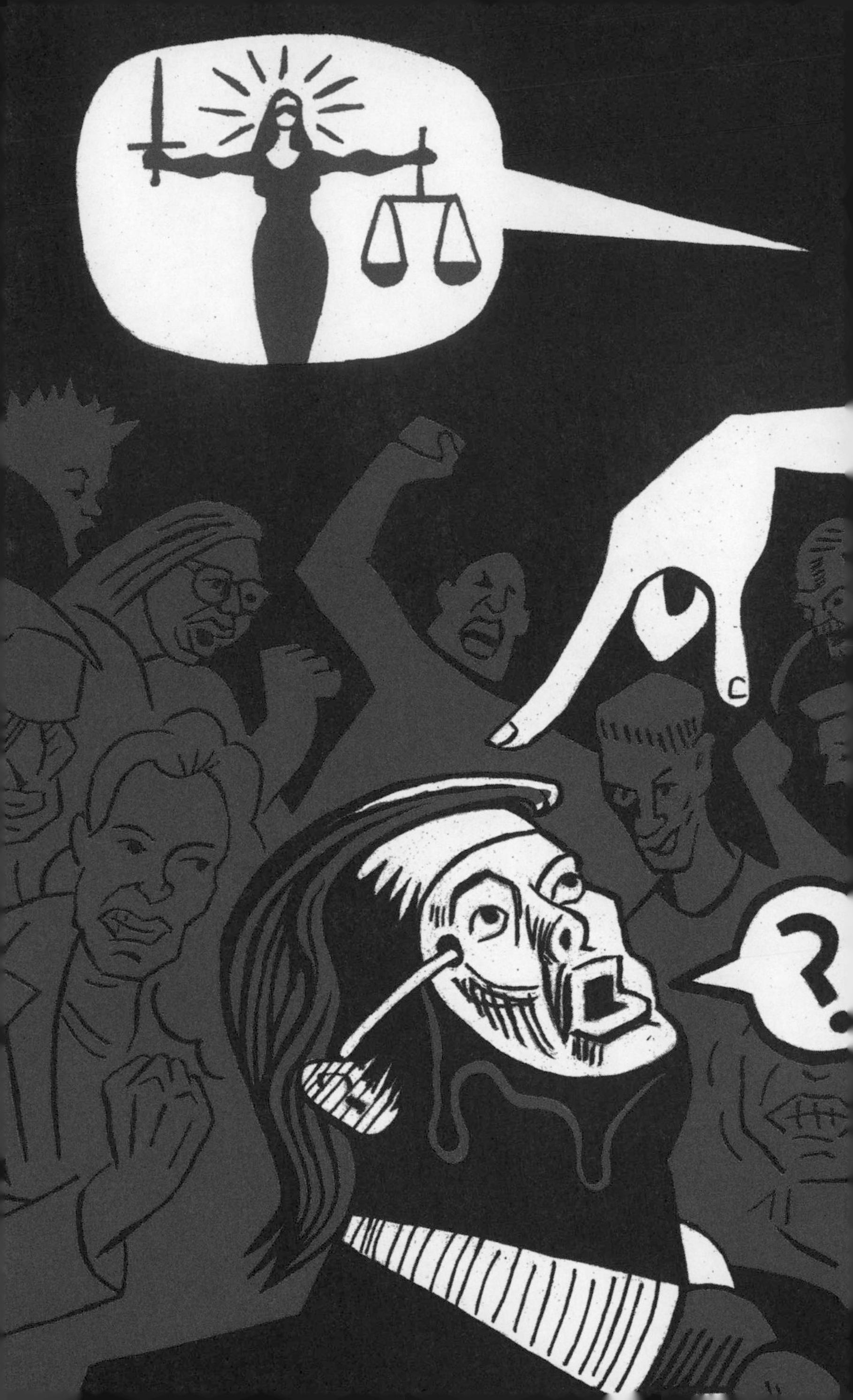

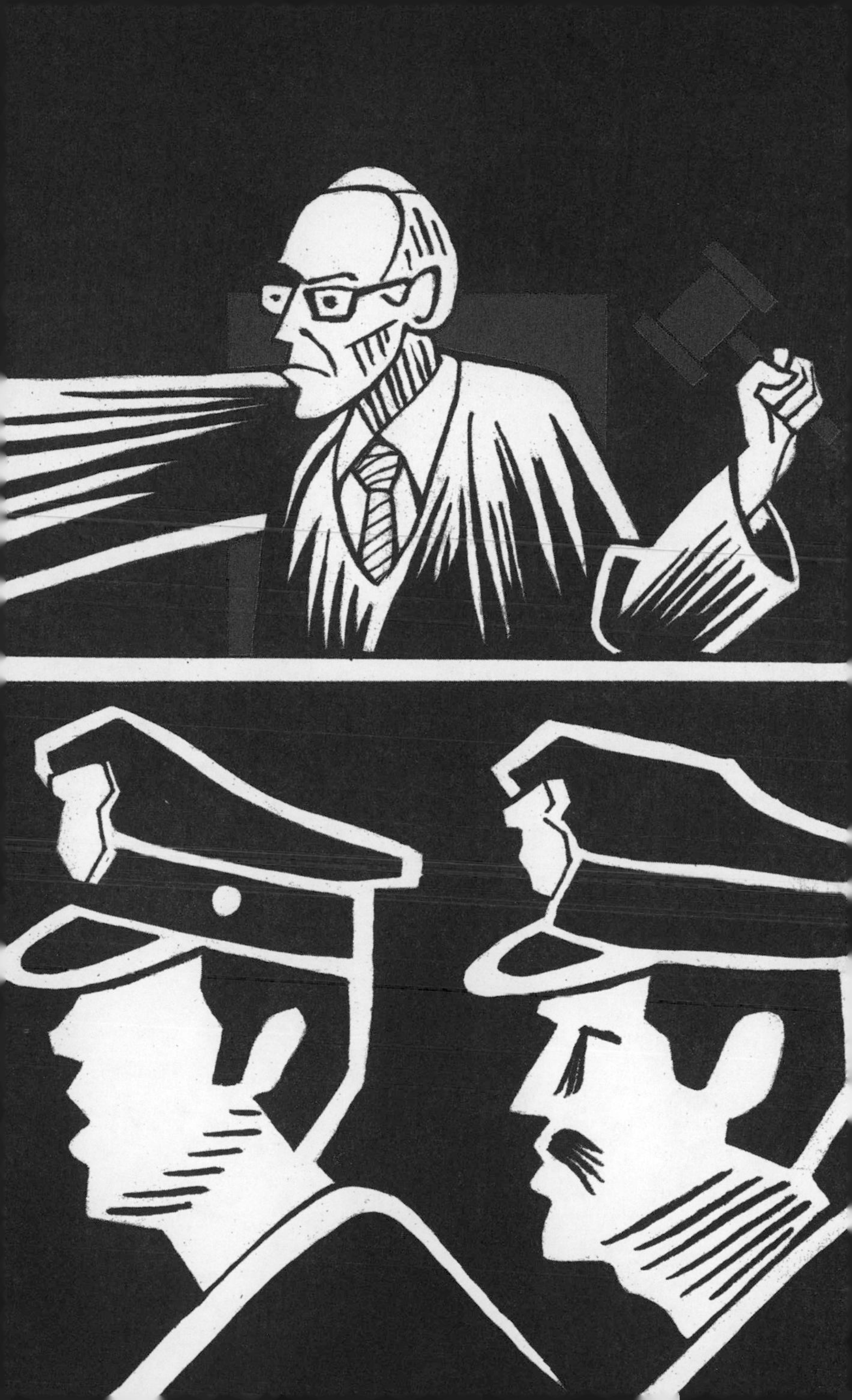

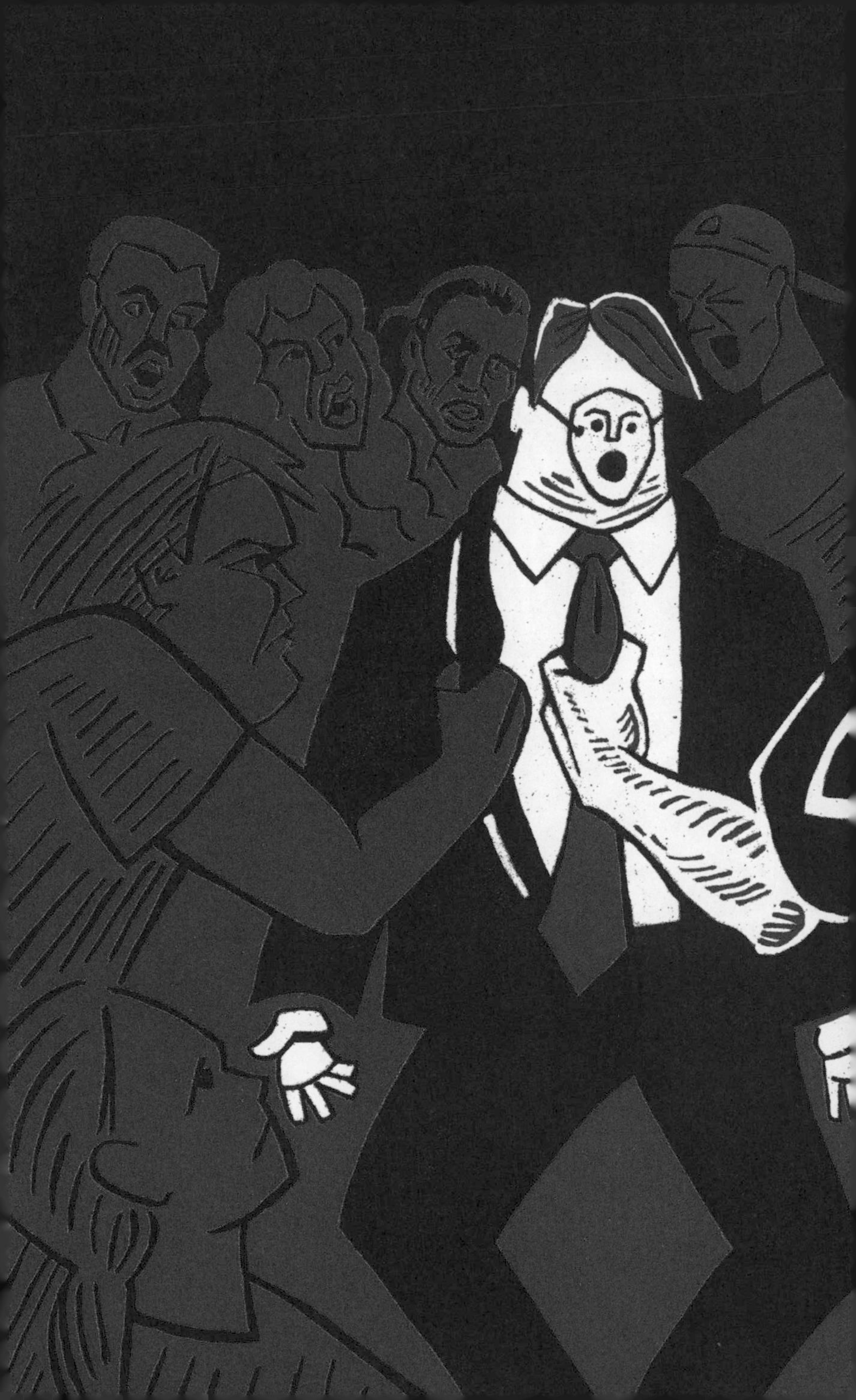

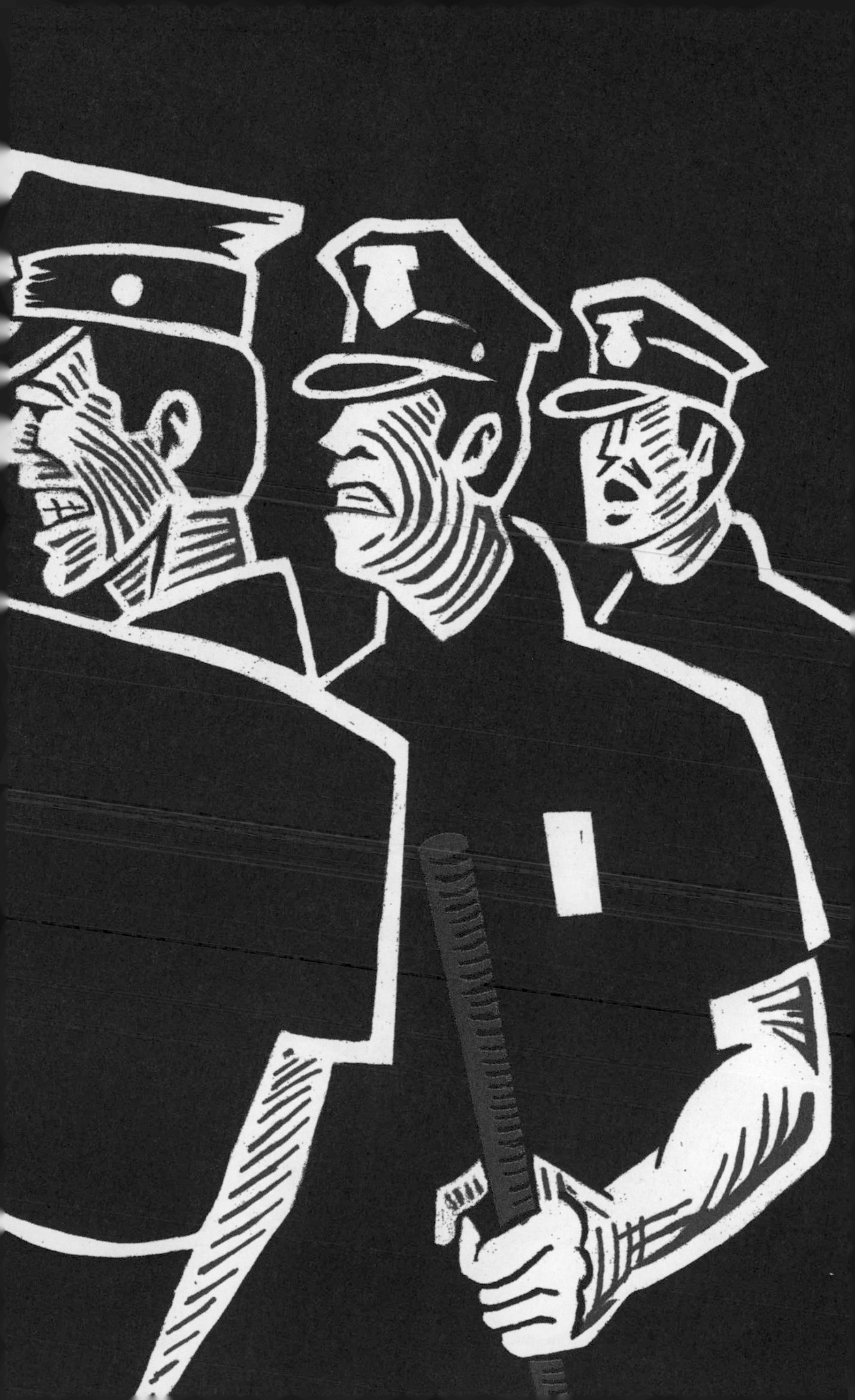

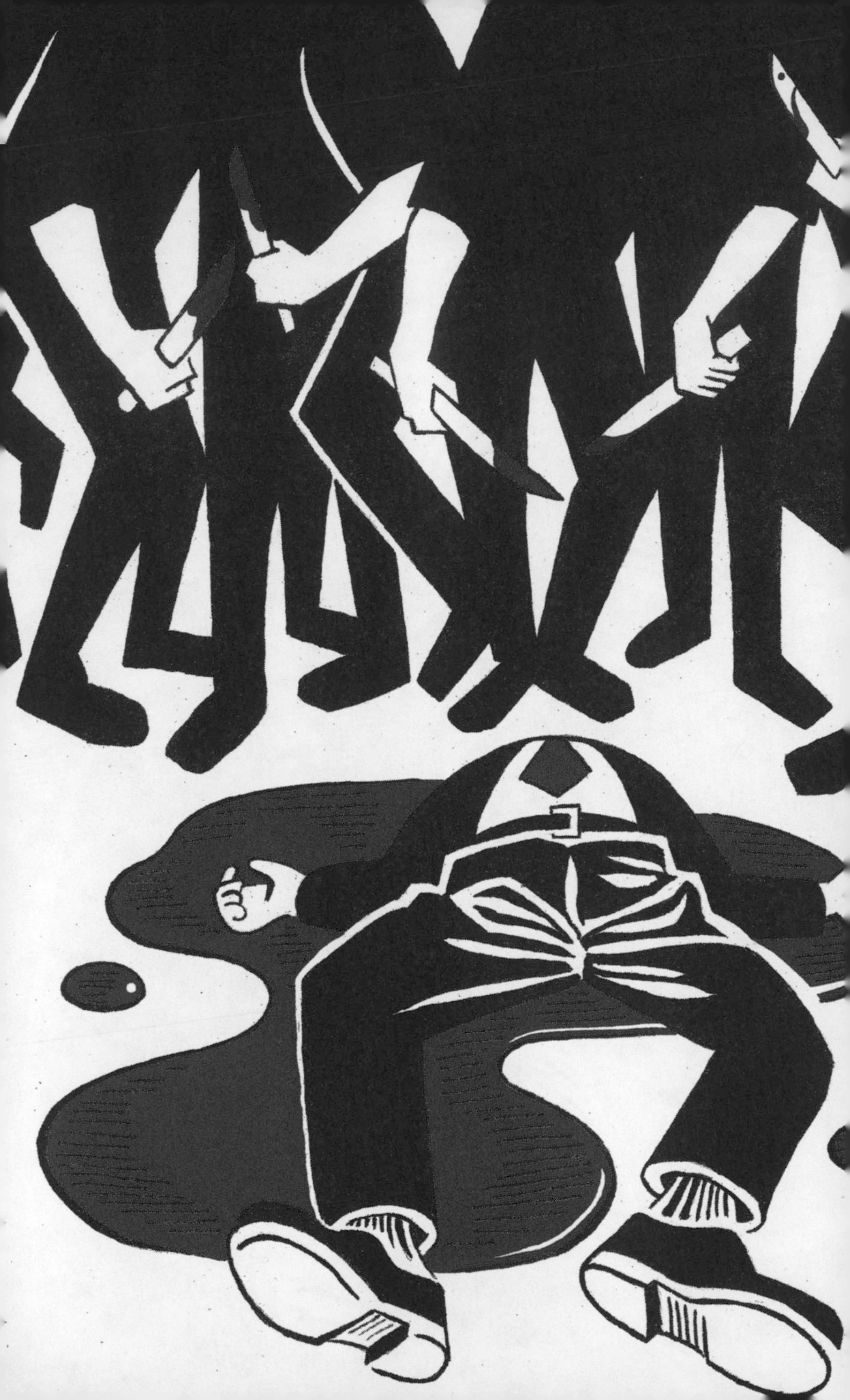

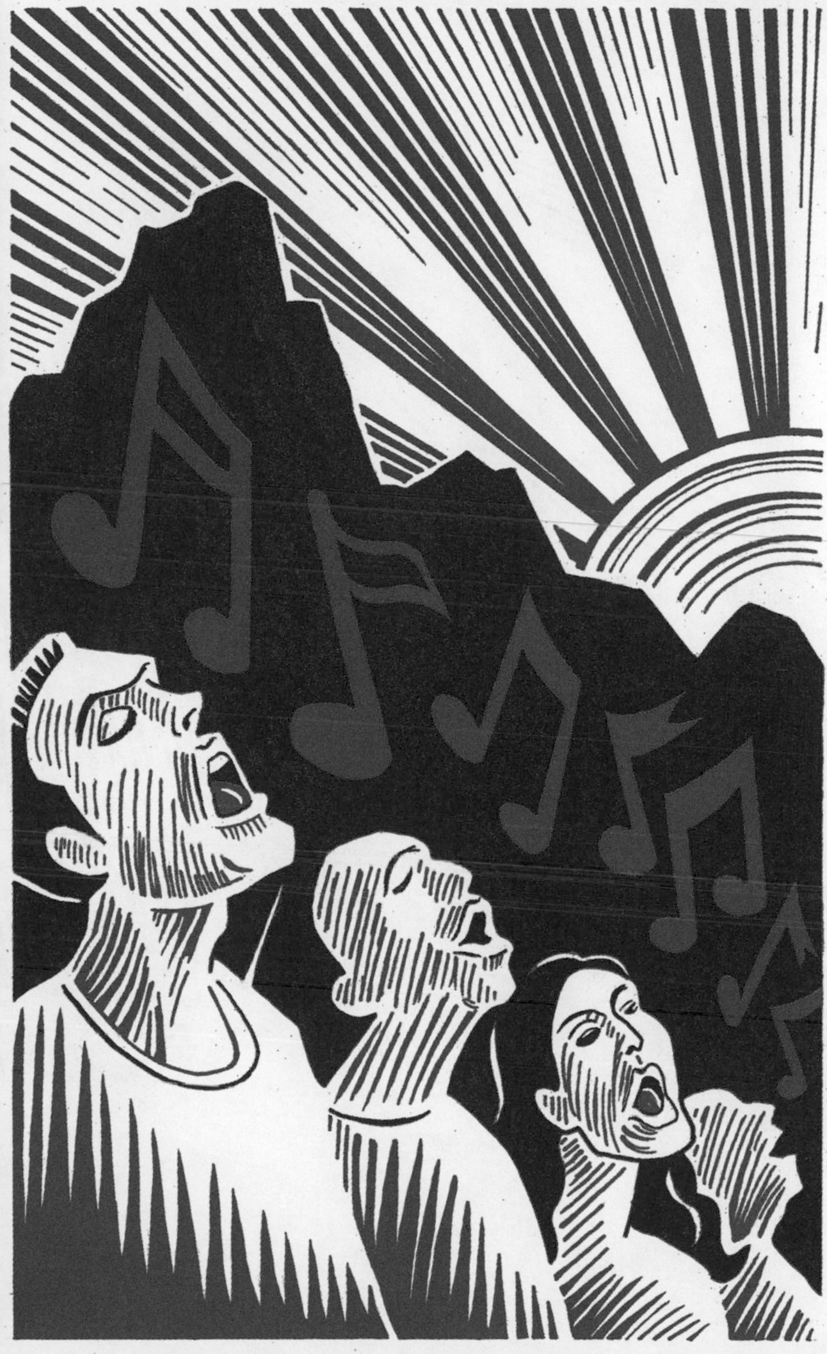

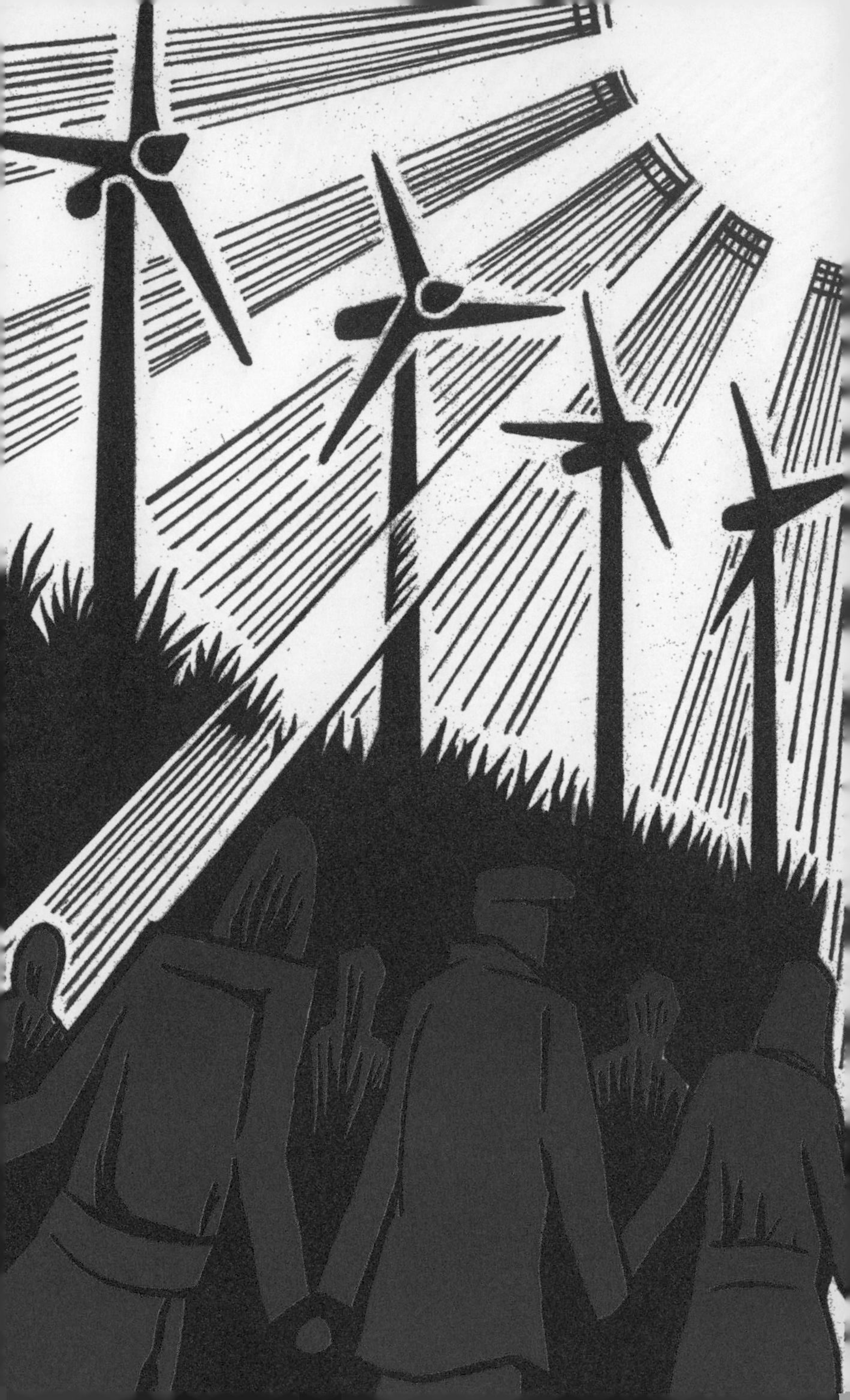

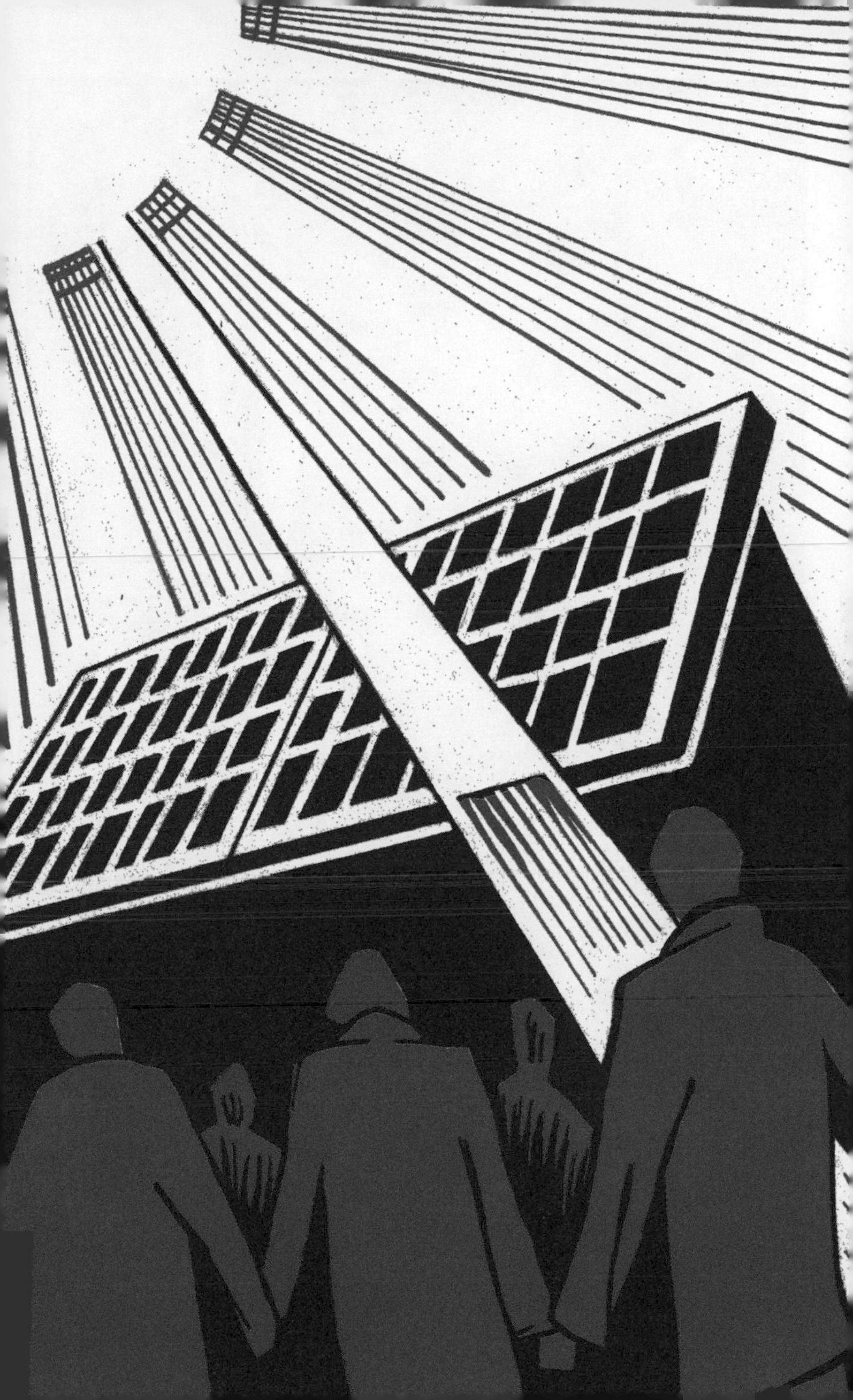

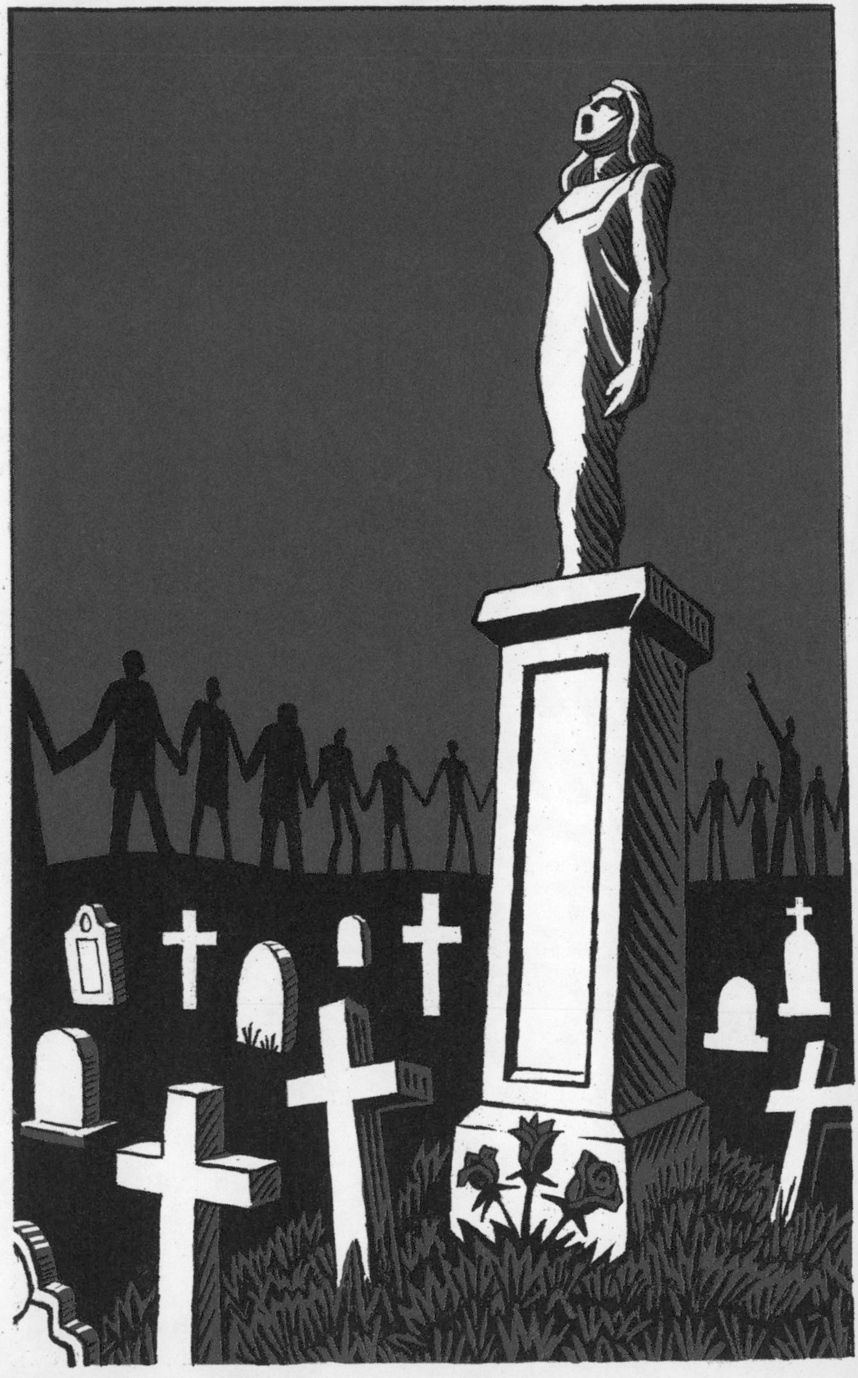

HOW THIS BOOK CAME ABOUT

In 2018, Paulin Dardel, an editor at the French publishing house CMDE, asked me to "create a parable of the rise of fascism, in the style of *The Idea* by Frans Masereel."

The "Idea" in Masereels's series of witty woodcuts, is a beautiful woman who pops out of an artists' head and goes running out into the world. I immediately understood that, in a contemporary version, the woman would have to be more than a man's fantasy. She would have to be a legitimate protagonist with ideas of her own.

But looking at *The Idea* also led me to meditate on how, throughout history, images of women have been used to signify important ideas. A practice that may have its origins in prehistoric goddess worship. Or the cause of this custom may be more quotidian. Perhaps artists have always drawn pictures of strong women because such women have always existed.

It also occurred to me that ideas are not the pristine things they may have appeared to be at the start of the twentieth century. Today we think of ideas as commodities in a marketplace. We speak of "intellectual property" and its dialectical antithesis "plagiarism."

Fascists are plagiarists. They steal ideas from the left in order to win the support of the masses. We have all witnessed how Donald Trump co-opted the populist rhetoric of Bernie Sanders and the anti-globalization analysis of revolutionary activists. We have seen him seize the slogan of the peace movement—"Say no to endless wars"—to justify his breathtakingly transactional foreign policies. The Republicans have even stolen the color red. What fascism produces is not so much an ideology, but a grotesque parody of politics, a Bizarro World, in which opposites are fused together and weaponized.

This book is an homage to the wordless books of Frans Masereel and Lynd Ward. But also to the work of their contemporaries, such as Thomas Hart Benton, Hugo Gellert, Käthe Kollwitz, and the Sawyer brothers, and to their predecessors such as Francisco Goya. Artists who offered a vision of human solidarity and secular morality, so absent today.

This book is a call to those of us who genuinely believe in ideas like universal human rights, world peace, and social justice, to remember who we are and to take back what has been stolen. Before it is too late.

Seth Tobocman
New York City, November 2019

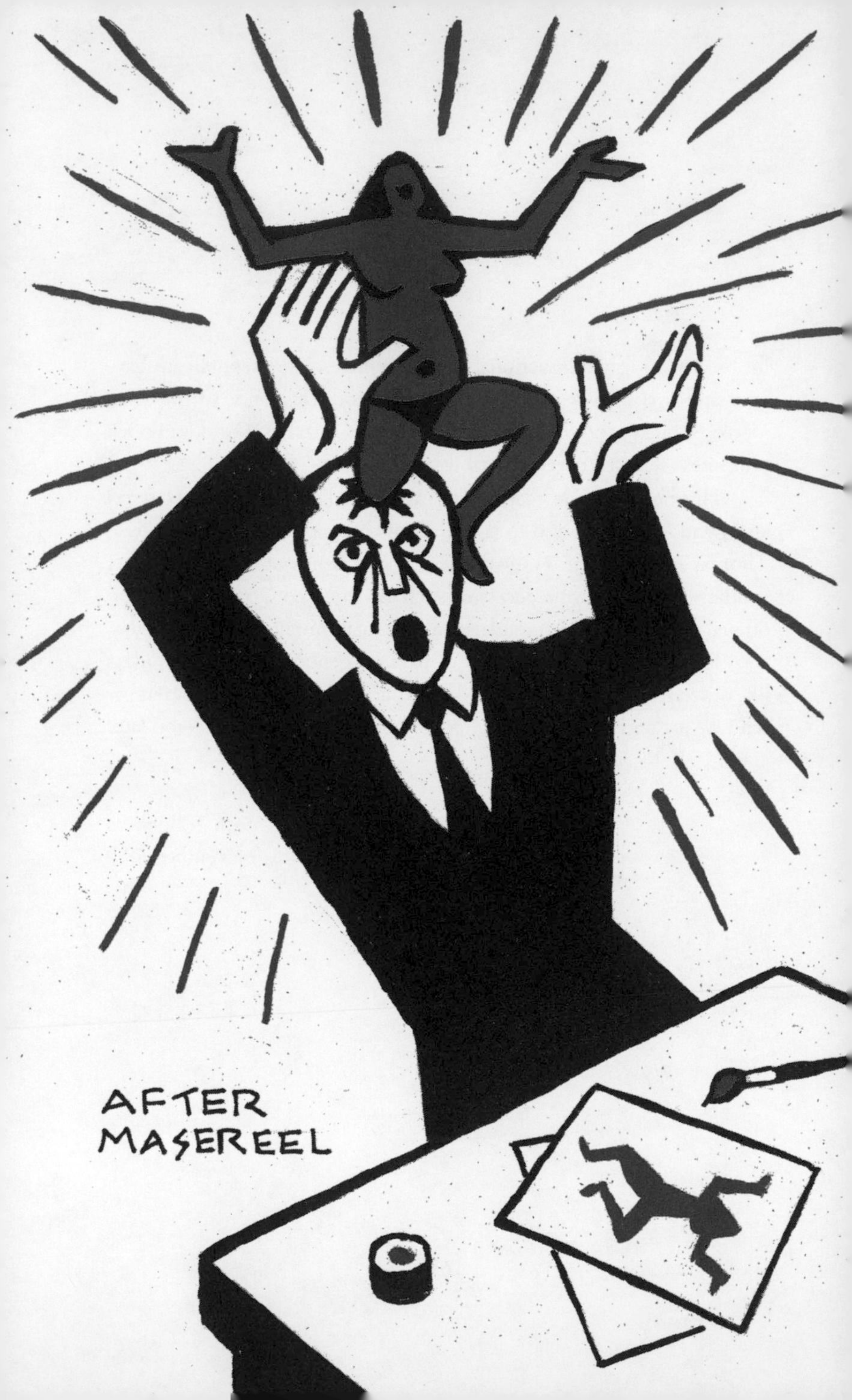
AFTER
MASEREEL

AFTER THE
VENUS OF
WILLENDORF

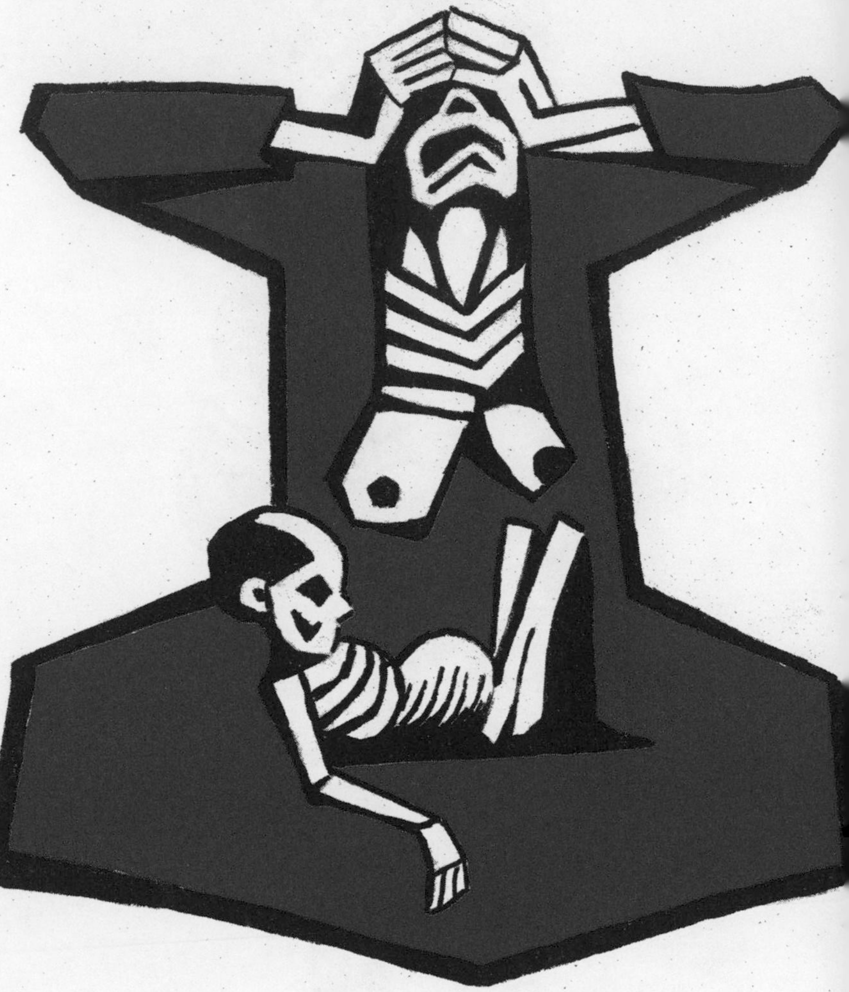

AFTER
KÄTHE
KOLLWITZ

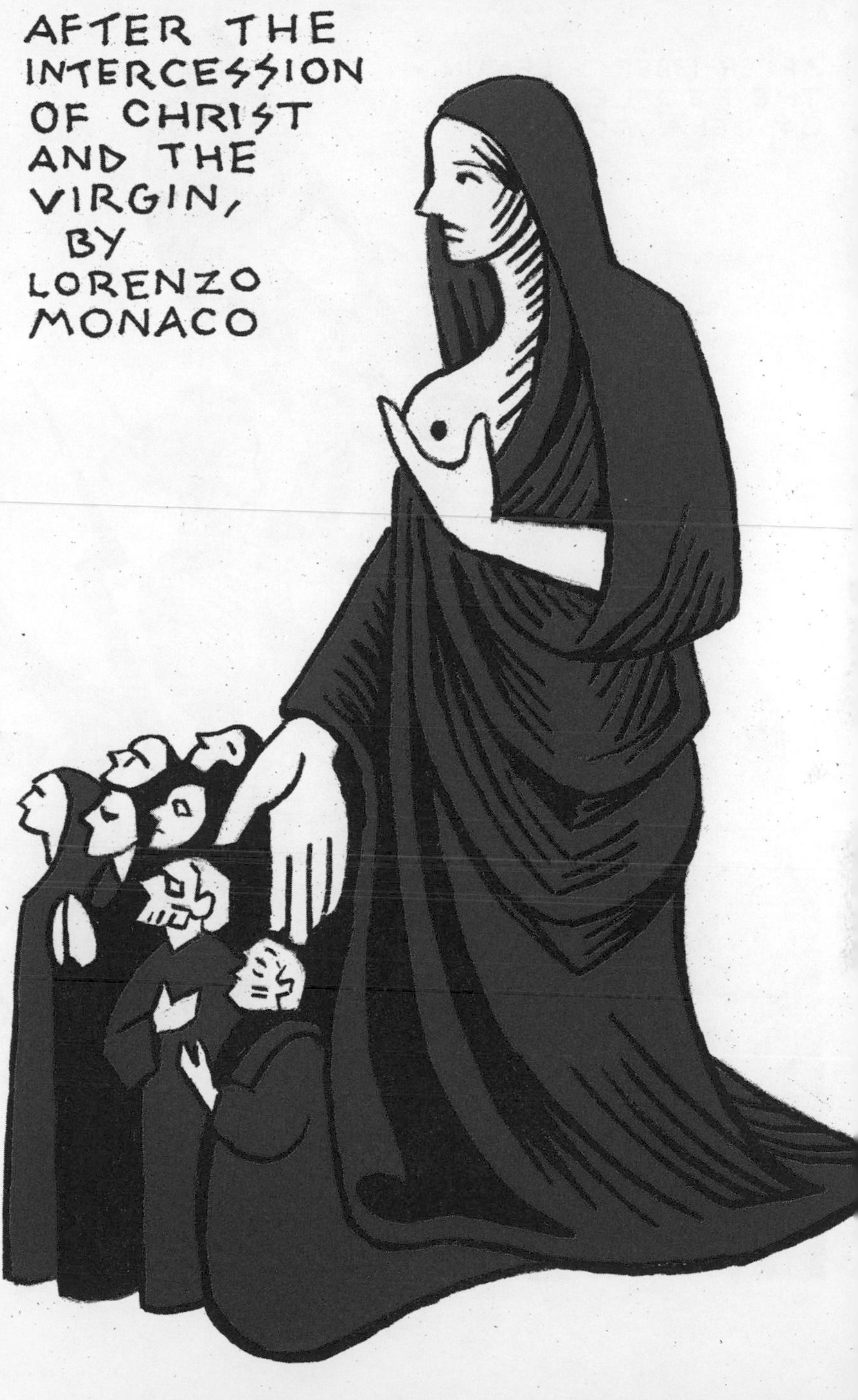
AFTER THE INTERCESSION OF CHRIST AND THE VIRGIN, BY LORENZO MONACO

AFTER LIBERTY LEADING THE PEOPLE, BY DELACROIX

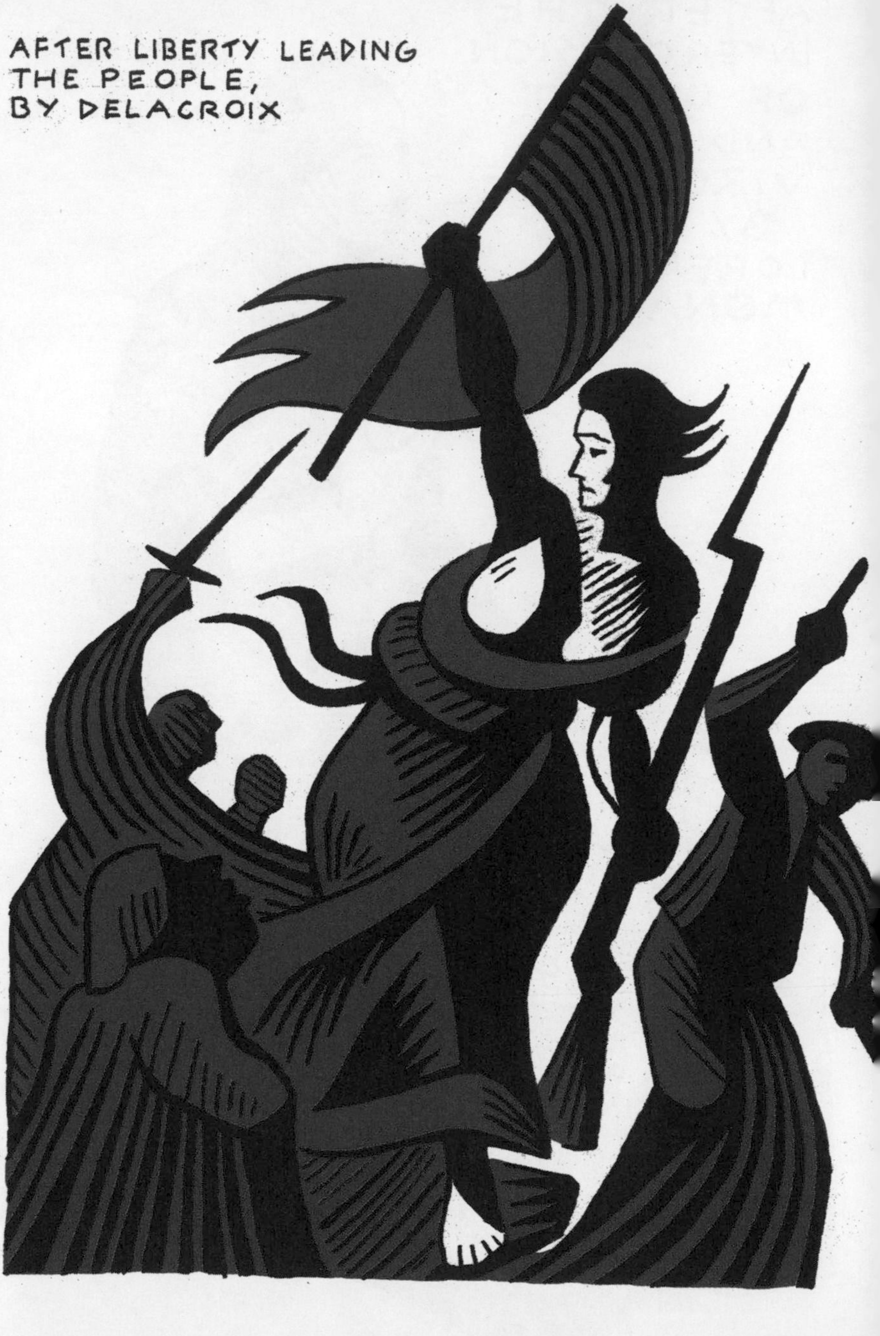

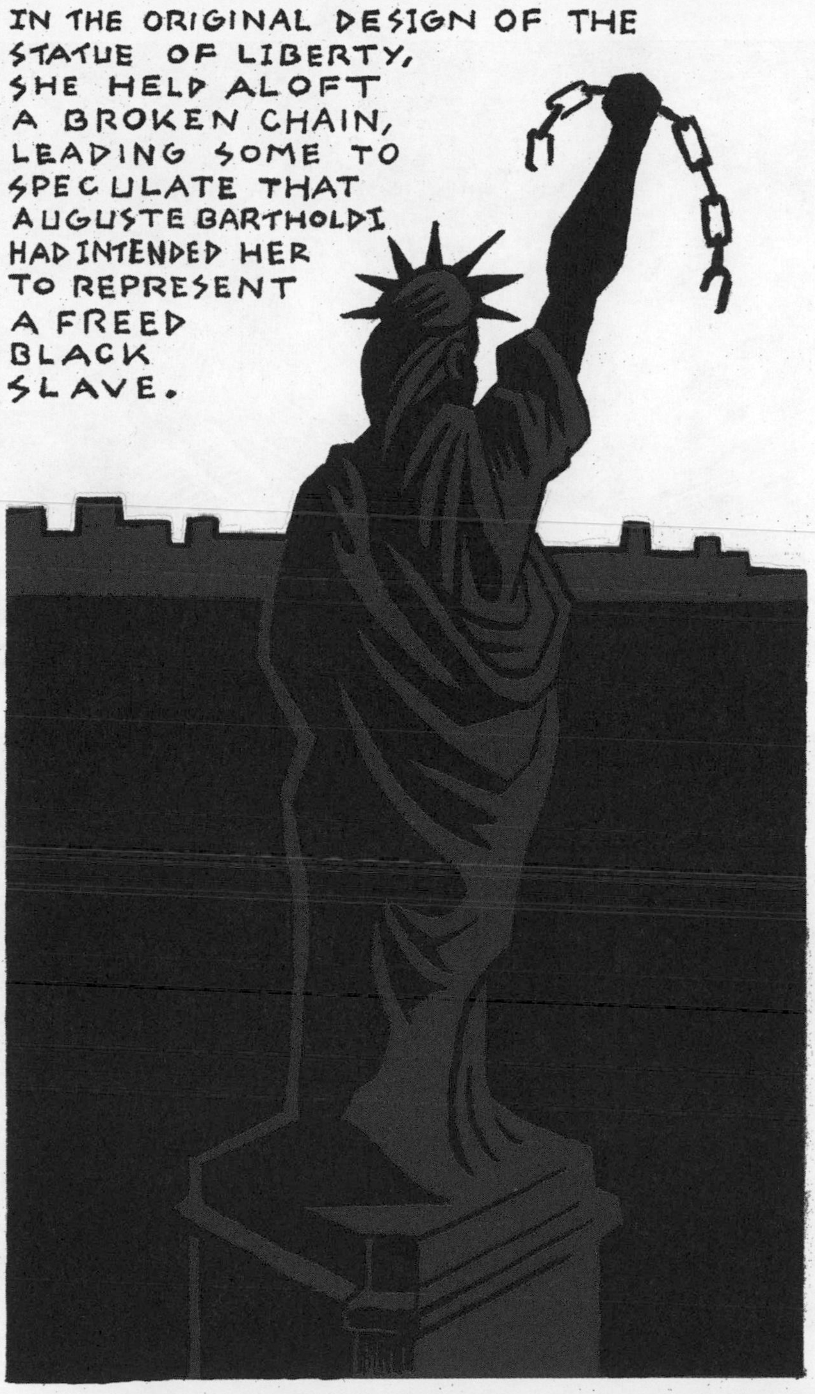
IN THE ORIGINAL DESIGN OF THE STATUE OF LIBERTY, SHE HELD ALOFT A BROKEN CHAIN, LEADING SOME TO SPECULATE THAT AUGUSTE BARTHOLDI HAD INTENDED HER TO REPRESENT A FREED BLACK SLAVE.

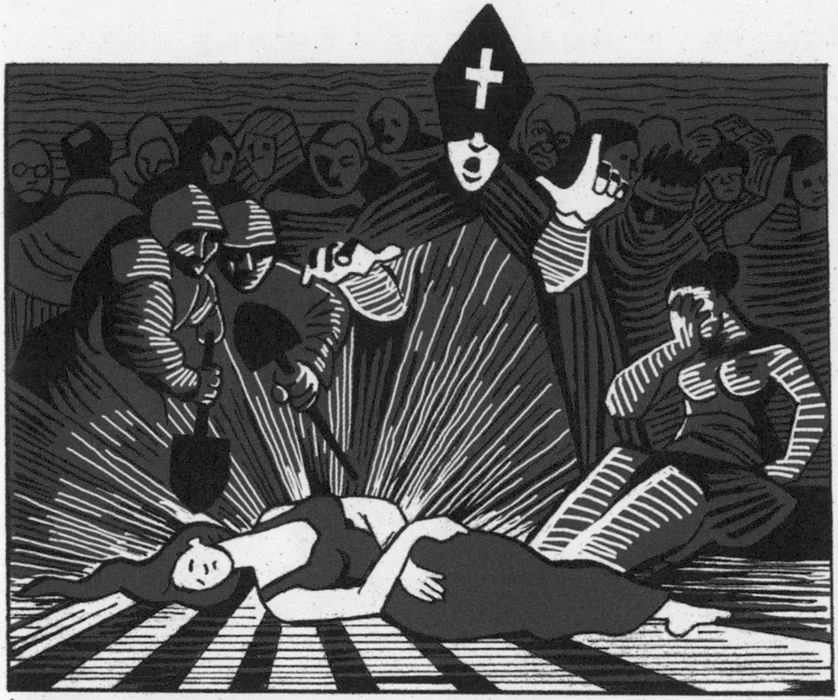

"THE TRUTH HAS DIED."

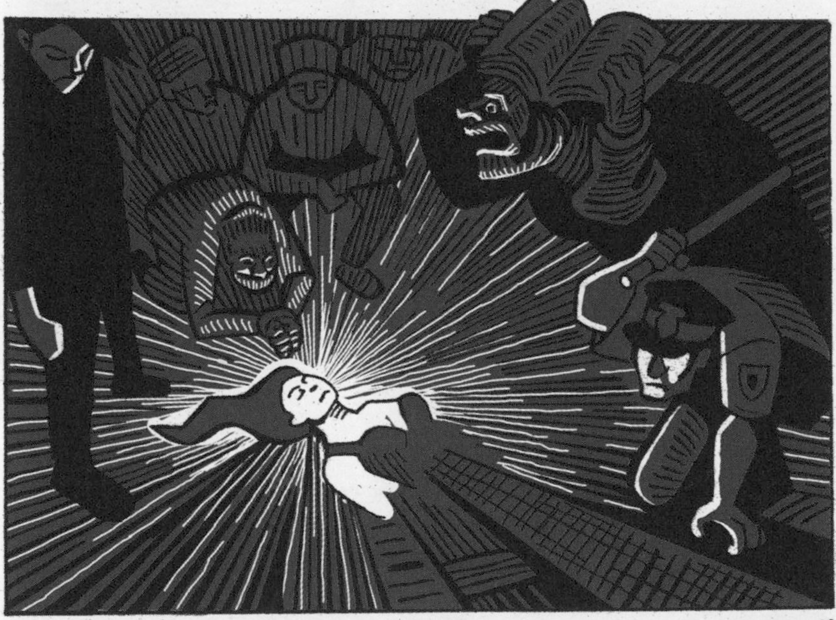

"WILL SHE LIVE AGAIN?"

"THIS IS THE TRUTH."

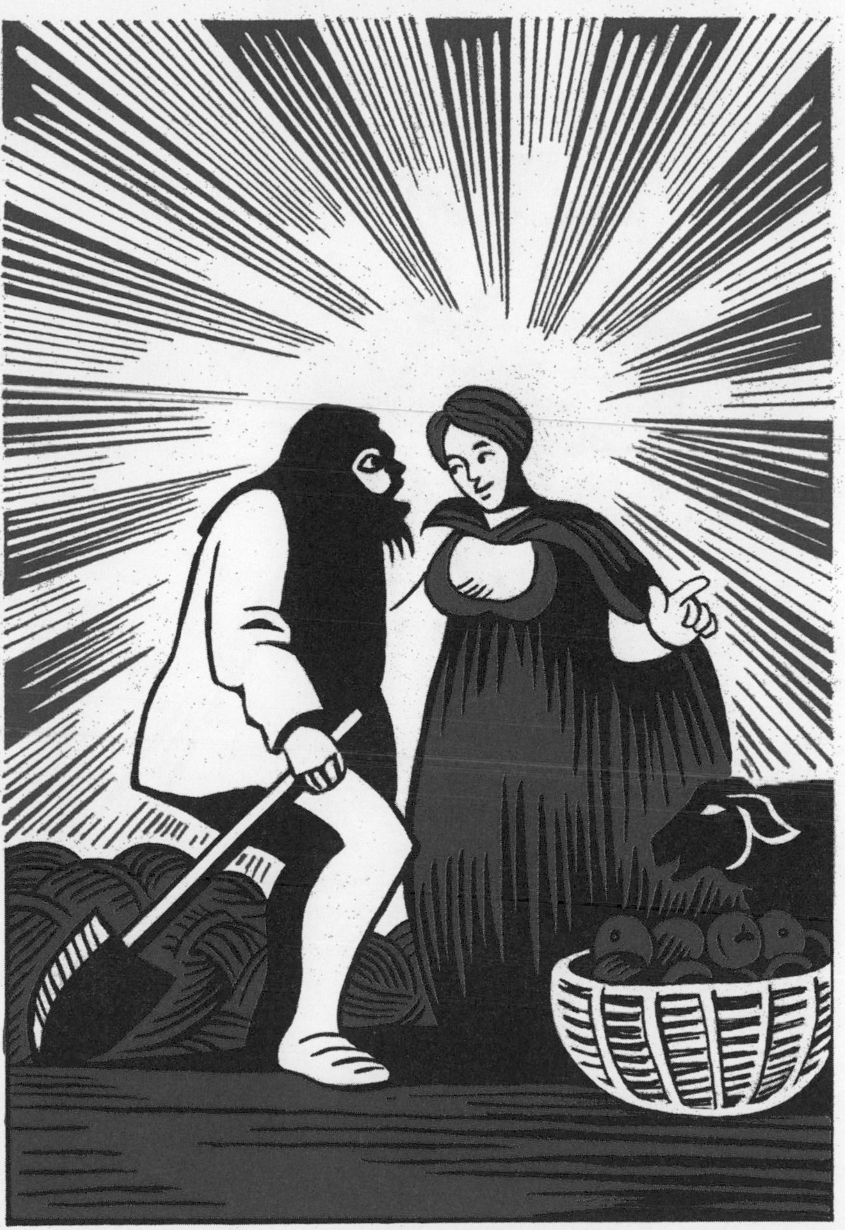

AFTER FRANCISCO GOYA

Seth Tobocman is a comic-book artist whose works include *You Don't Have to Fuck People Over to Survive*, *War in the Neighborhood*, and *Disaster and Resistance*.

Peter Kuper is a comic-book artist and author of *The System*, *Drawn to New York*, and an illustrated edition of Kafka's *The Metamorphosis*.